EXIT THE MAZE

One Addiction,
One Cause,
One Cure

DR. DONNA MARKS

Exit the Maze: One Addiction, One Cause, One Cure

Published by Westward Publishing
West Palm Beach, FL

ISBN: 978-0-578-59545-0

SELF-HELP / Addiction

Cover and Interior Design by Nick Zelinger

QUANTITY PURCHASES:
Schools, companies, professional groups, clubs, and other organizations may qualify for special terms when ordering quantities of this title. For information, email drdonnamarks@gmail.com.

Printed in the United States of America

CONTENTS

THE ADDICTION MAZE

A rat in a maze is free to go anywhere,
as long as it stays inside the maze.
—Margaret Atwood

When we think of a maze, most of us think of a fun puzzle that we did as children. It had an entrance and an exit, and the only goal was to find your way out. You'd draw a line through a series of corridors to find the exit, which often was located at the perimeter on an opposite side of the maze. Your pencil line might have hit a few dead ends, and you might even have become a little frustrated, but through trial and error, you'd learn to see the paths that didn't work and find your way through.

Another type of maze is one I encountered in a psychology class. We used the maze to test the behavior of mice and how they learn. These mazes were three-dimensional, so the dead ends were blocked by walls, not just lines drawn on paper. Research scientists would do experiments with mice in mazes that included rewards such as food, punishments such as an electric shock, or a combination of both. In some cases, the mice would keep hitting a lever to get morphine or running to-and-fro in the maze to get a reward. The mouse would pursue the goal and, depending on how badly it wanted the reward, sometimes do so to the point of pain or exhaustion.

Addiction behavior operates like a hungry mouse looking for cheese in a maze. The mouse frantically runs through the maze in all different directions looking for the cheese. The mouse doesn't care about the amount, the shape of the cheese, or its flavor. No matter what, it will race up and down the maze searching. Even if the mouse is shocked with electric current every time it eats the cheese, it may be traumatized, but presented with the opportunity, the mouse will still go after the cheese. Obsessed with getting the cheese, the mouse never seeks the exit out of the maze.

A person caught in the maze of addiction is similar to the mouse in that the addict will continue to seek out the "cheese" (a metaphor for any addictive substance or behavior) in spite of negative feedback, no matter how punishing it becomes. Like the mouse looking for cheese, the addicted person will continue to run the maze, frantically searching for the next "reward" or fix. This has become a massive social problem.

Although addicts often are shamed for their behavior, addiction is not something to be ashamed of. It is a symptom of a greater problem that the person didn't create. In modern societies, people have been conditioned to take a pill for just about everything. When a person feels anxious or depressed, the doctor prescribes a pill, sometimes in tandem with counseling, but often not. There are more than 20 million adults in the United States diagnosed with anxiety[1] and another 17.3 million adults who've suffered at least one bout of depression.[2] In the last two years, 25 million people in the United States have taken antidepressants, 15 million have been on them for more than five years, and many have found themselves unable to stop due to the side effects,[3] such as headaches, dizziness, nausea, and mood swings[4]—the same as for many other addictive drug withdrawals.

Of the thousands of people with whom I have worked, every person I've seen has either been addicted or had a family member or loved one who was. I want to change your perception of addiction from something wrong with you to something that's wrong with our conditioning. We live in a society that unconsciously attempts to replace love with endless substitutes. If you are struggling with addiction, know that you are not alone. You are one of millions paying the price for a society malnourished of love.

More than half of all deaths in the United States are related to heart disease or cancer,[5] often caused by abusing the body by some form of (diagnosed or undiagnosed) addiction.

---

[1] "Any Anxiety Disorder," National Institute of Mental Health, updated November 2017, nimh.nih.gov/health/statistics/any-anxiety-disorder.shtml.
[2] "Major Depression," National Institute of Mental Health, updated February 2019, nimh.nih.gov/health/statistics/major-depression.shtml.
[3] Benedict Carey and Robert Gebeloff, "Many People Taking Antidepressants Discover They Can't Quit," NYTimes.com, April 7, 2018, www.nytimes.com/2018/04/07/health/antidepressants-withdrawal-prozac-cymbalta.html.
[4] Lee Weber, "Can You Get Addicted to Antidepressants?" Addiction Blog, February 16, 2012, prescription-drug.addictionblog.org/can-you-get-addicted-to-antidepressants/.
[5] "Leading Causes of Death," CDC/National Center for Health Statistics, reviewed March 17, 2017, www.cdc.gov/nchs/fastats/leading-causes-of-death.htm.

Heart and lung diseases, cancers, and diabetes are the world's largest killers, with an estimated 38 million deaths annually.[6] In the United States alone, well over 100 million people suffer from addiction. According to the research, there are 15.1 million alcohol abusers,[7] 11.1 million opiate abusers,[8] 10 million with gambling disorders,[9] 50 million addicted to nicotine,[10] 70 million addicted to food,[11] 9 million engaged in sex addiction,[12] and 20 million shopping addicts.[13] If you add up even the few numbers listed here, it represents more than half the U.S. population. Note that these numbers do not include those addicted to illegal drugs, video gaming, exercise, work, or any other type of compulsive behavior that can rule a person's life. The type of fix doesn't matter; the brain has one goal—dopamine—the neurotransmitter that creates a sense of pleasure.

[6] Samanada Dorger, "The Leading Causes of Death in the World," *TheStreet*, February 26, 2019, www.thestreet.com/world/leading-causes-of-death-world-14869811.

[7] "Alcohol Facts and Statistics," National Institute on Alcohol Abuse and Alcoholism, updated August 2018, www.niaaa.nih.gov/alcohol-facts-and-statistics.

[8] Beth Han et al. "Prescription Opioid Use, Misuse, and Use Disorders in U.S. Adults: 2015 National Survey on Drug Use and Health," *Annals of Internal Medicine*, September 5, 2017, annals.org/aim/article-abstract/2646632/prescription-opioid-use-misuse-use-disorders-u-s-adults-2015.

[9] "Statistics of Gambling Addiction 2016," North American Foundation for Gambling Addiction Help, nafgah.org/statistics-gambling-addiction-2016/.

[10] Neal L. Benowitz, "Nicotine Addiction," *PubMed Central*, August 25, 2010, www.ncbi.nlm.nih.gov/pmc/articles/PMC2928221/.

[11] Michael Candelaria, "Food Addiction Numbers Rising," *OrlandoSentinel.com*, September 2, 2016, www.orlandosentinel.com/health/os-food-addiction-numbers-rising-20160902-story.html.

[12] Nadine DeNinno, "Sex Addiction Epidemic: Study Finds 9 Million Americans Are Sex Addicts," *International Business Times*, November 30, 2011, www.ibtimes.com/sex-addiction-epidemic-study-finds-9-million-americans-are-sex-addicts-376908.

[13] "Are You One of 20 Million Shopping Addicts in America?" *ProjectKnow.com*, American Addiction Centers, Inc., www.projectknow.com/are-you-one-of-americas-20-million-shopping-addicts/.

Often when I give a public speech, I ask all of the people who have children to raise their hands. I ask them, "If any of you have given your six-month-old baby a cigarette, raise your hand." Of course, no one has raised their hand. Then I ask, "How many of you have given your baby a shot of whiskey? A Valium? A bag of sugar? Six shots of espresso? A little heroin?"

Everyone chuckles, then I ask, "Then why do you suppose you started putting those very things in your own body?"

Dead silence.

The time has come to break that silence and to start answering the question, "Why?" Why are we like mice running in a maze? How did we get here? Why do we stay in the maze? How do we get out?

My Own Journey

I remember one evening when I was about five years old sitting in my animal-print pajamas next to my grandmother watching television. My teddy bear was tucked under one arm while I sucked my thumb on the other hand. A commercial came on that captured my attention. A thin, beautiful woman in a shirtwaist dress leaned against a tree and gazed at her beau. She held a long, slender Salem cigarette, just like the one my grandmother held in her hand that very moment. That ad branded in my mind that menthol cigarettes were the source of serenity and romance.

It didn't stop there. I drank the sugary Kool-Aid that "made playtime more fun," and I wanted the newest doll or anything else that offered the promise of fun and escape. It never occurred to me that I was being programmed to believe that the ugliness I felt, inside and out, could be swept away with those products.

As the level of pain and trauma (from emotional, physical, and sexual abuse) I endured at home increased, I gradually forgot the other things that had lifted me and filled me with inspiration—ballet, music, swimming, nature, and the little voice inside that helped me understand there was something wrong in my house, and it wasn't me. But it took time to do ballet, music, and swimming. And to hear that little reassuring voice, I needed at least a moment of quiet and feeling of safety to connect. Eventually, my emotional turmoil increased faster than I could cope.

I first entered the addiction maze at age twelve, when I was offered a Salem cigarette at a slumber party. My lungs warned me with the violent cough, but the instantaneous altered state that auto-clicked in my brain overrode the harm I was doing to my body. I never intended to smoke the whole carton in one night, but that's exactly what I did. The subtle emotional numbing and the sudden sense of belonging to a girl tribe gave me a feeling of connection I'd never experienced before. The next day, the tribe was gone, but getting another cigarette was the predominant thought in my mind. Despite the foul odor and horrible aftertaste, I felt compelled to re-experience the calming euphoria that first drag had provided. The nicotine corridor in the maze formed around me and continued to expand over the years. I'd buy cigarettes from a vending machine, steal them from my grandparents' packs, or bum them from a friend, then when confronted, I'd adamantly deny ever smoking. After a few years, realizing my conscience and free will had been hijacked, I would decide to quit, every day. But I'd forget to stop, put it off until the next day, or quit for a few days then start again. Twice I stopped for several months, but then after a crisis, I'd smoke "just one," under the illusion that I could stop at that.

When it came to drinking, however, I was careful to limit my intake. After all, I grew up in an alcoholic household and vowed I would never drink like my stepfather, who consumed a couple of cases of beer in a day. But over time, my resolve wore thin, and I drank with abandon, losing myself further into the maze. After a suicide attempt at age fifteen, I met my first psychiatrist, and like the next three, he knew nothing about addictions or its effects on children.

By age sixteen, I was married, with an infant, waitressing, and going to night school to get my high school diploma. By age eighteen, I was divorced and struggling to survive. Survive I did, from one crisis to the next. Amid the chaos, that same inner voice from youth told me I could do better and inspired me to go to college and work my way into a better life. I spent the next twelve years dedicating myself to my education and training to become a therapist. In spite of all that, it wasn't enough to help me heal, and the inner divide between addiction and mental health remained.

The alcohol corridor led me to seek other halls with other mood-altering experiences. It didn't matter what they were as long as there was the possibility of reliving that first mind-blowing hit of nicotine. Every addict chases that first rush of *aahhhh*, but the addiction never delivers. Each attempt only lures us deeper into the maze.

When I was thirty years old, the impact of addiction on my life became untenable, and I had to get out. After my second divorce, I added marijuana and a new on-and-off addictive relationship to my nicotine and alcohol habits. That's when I had another emotional crash. This time I went to an addiction counselor who referred me to treatment. Relieved of chemical dependency, I thought I was cured. I did not know I remained in the addiction maze.

I unconsciously pursued whatever route would help me escape myself. Workaholism seemed like a good choice because I made money. But I began to make work more important than time with my children and taking time alone to regroup. Love and sex seemed normal enjoyments, but neither lasted, and I ping-ponged from one failed marriage to the next. Marathon running and long-distance bicycling were good for my health and provided a "natural" high, but if I didn't get that endorphin rush, I suffered the same irritability and moodiness of jonesing as with any addiction. Shopping seemed a harmless distraction, except I had no savings. I also became a recovery and spirituality junkie. I'd always get a blip of relief from the latest book or seminar, but the feeling never lasted. There remained an emptiness inside that nothing could fill.

Eventually, I got addicted to getting better. I turned myself inside out with every imaginable form of therapy. Gestalt therapy helped rid me of backed up rage toward my step-father. Biofeedback and hypnotherapy taught me how to relax and stay calm. Cognitive therapy helped me remain rational during upsets. Psychoanalysis offered my first chance at a relationship that supported me through buckets of tears, and for the first time, in my forties, I learned how to trust another human being. Each modality helped pieces of me, but the messages were mixed. The mental health counselors didn't understand addiction, the addiction counselors didn't understand mental health, and neither understood my spiritual void. I remained unhealed.

I scoured the globe in search of spiritual guidance. Church felt more like a business than a place to connect, but I tried and tried. I studied the 12 Steps, Buddhism, Christian Science, Kabbalah, shamanism, Yoga. Most of the so-called spiritual gurus I encountered were charlatans. I paid enormous fees to listen to charismatic jargon and sound effects amid razzle-dazzle lighting only to discover later that these leaders did not walk the talk.

Confused and disillusioned, I walked away from everything—recovery, spirituality, therapy. And then like the prodigal child, I came back. There had to be a way, and I had to figure it out.

After much contemplation, I recognized that my life had become a jumble of many different mega-puzzles with all the pieces thrown together in one giant bag. Now, before I could get well, I had to put it all down, sit with myself, and gather and organize the pieces that created the picture of the life I wanted to live and eliminate the rest.

The first piece was sobriety; without that, nothing else could fall into place. I returned to recovery meetings with a whole new attitude, starting with gratitude rather than a judgment about the imperfections of the program. Next, I had to get right spiritually. I was mad at God because I'd worked so hard to heal myself, and I blamed my failure on that unseen entity rather than my own self-will. I returned to prayer, meditation, and A Course in Miracles with a deeper commitment than just going through the motions—this time, without my own agenda, I was entitled to nothing but free will. I recognized that true freedom comes from embracing life on its terms, not by pursuing my selfish desires.

Next, I reviewed all of the therapy I'd experienced and extrapolated from each modality that had worked in my healing process. Happiness came in a flash, and this time, it stayed. In spite of my many prior failures and careless mistakes, an inner strength took hold. A new sense of confidence replaced the void and pain that previously had sent me in all the wrong directions. For the first time in my life, I felt at peace.

Within a year, everything for which I'd striven so hard and now surrendered came about. I was relieved of burdensome business obligations that I'd carried for years. Lost friendships were restored. My first healthy relationship evolved into the kind of marriage I'd always longed for—a loving partnership supported by emotional availability and healthy problem-solving.

If you can relate to any of this, I implore you to read on. You are not alone.

The Addiction Epidemic

Our society has a massive addiction problem, but it can be solved. It won't be solved with new laws, pseudo help, or a war on drugs. Hundreds of millions of people are suffering from addiction, costing billions of dollars and millions of lives each year, yet the problem only grows. Many people are unaware they are addicted, or they know they're addicted, but they don't know why they feel worse when they stop. Or maybe, like me, they've searched their whole lives and were led in many directions, and when things didn't get better, they temporarily gave up.

Setbacks are never a reason to give up. We must never relent; we need only learn, then do better. I wrote this book to help those in the addiction maze find the exit as quickly as possible, without wasting years of time and thousands of dollars.

I also write with the hope that this book will contribute to my big vision goal: that by 2030, at least one million lives will be saved and not lost to addiction. I believe one crucial step— and what I am hoping to do with this book—is to change our current perspective on addiction and publicize the best way to prevent and cure addiction for good. Once people begin to accept that we have been looking at and treating addiction through primitive and ineffective models, we could reroute the billions of government and private dollars allotted to *fighting* addiction and apply those funds to *real prevention and cure*. If taken on globally, the approach offered in this book could eradicate addiction.

As you are about to find out, I believe there is only one addiction and one cure. I will explain more throughout these pages, but suffice it to say for now, that until we approach addiction in this manner, millions of addicted people who want a cure will continue to suffer and fail. They will either give up one addictive behavior and find a substitute, or they will go from one form of treatment to the next without healing the underlying cause. Most likely, they will do both, but neither is an addiction cure.

The method of treatment I will offer you in the following pages both exposes the one addiction for what it is and provides the cure.

Whether you are someone who is looking for a way out of addiction or you are a professional who wants to better serve your patients, I wrote this book for you. I can tell you from decades of personal experience and working with thousands of patients, there is a path to freedom from addiction and suffering. If you are willing to follow the guidance, you can exit the maze of addiction *forever*.

I suggest you approach the exercises in this book with a commitment and desire like none other to heal. Nothing will work without a desire to get well. Plan to move through the material gradually. It may take weeks or even months to read the material and do the exercises at the end of each chapter. I suggest you buy yourself a nice journal to keep your answers in one place, so you can turn to and reflect on them as you come to better understand yourself.

Give yourself the gift of taking time to digest the contents and wait until you've reached a sense of calm understanding before you go on to the next section. Equally important, no matter how much you might think you know already, read with an open mind and heart. Many of us know a lot, but we haven't learned a thing. The information provided is based on healing techniques that do work, but only when you implement them and follow through.

If you are like most people who struggle with addiction, you probably had a vision for your life, but something interrupted that dream, and life pulled you into a different paradigm. Imagine right now what your life would look like if you were living your greatest childhood dreams. The following pages can bring you back to yourself, the life you were meant to have, and the person you were meant to be. If you're stuck in the maze and you want to get out, now is the time. Somewhere in the maze, there is an exit sign, and my intention is to help you find it.

PART I

ONE ADDICTION

To overcome the addiction epidemic, the first thing we need to let go of is the idea that there are multiple addictions. The truth is there is only one. It's time to stop fooling around with people's lives and get right to the point. Addiction is addiction. We need to recognize that once someone has become addicted, simply ending an addictive behavior does not mean that the specific addiction is cured. It means only that the behavior has stopped.

Let's use alcoholism as an example. An alcoholic stops drinking. They faithfully attend AA meetings, get their chip, and stay in touch with their sponsor, all great things to do. But just as often, alcoholics simultaneously take up a "new" addiction, whether it be sugar, sex, caffeine, nicotine, etc. When this is the case, why do we say these people are "on the wagon"? Are they really "sober"? I say no; they are still under the influence of addiction, still trapped in the maze, and it's high time we start to acknowledge that they are using a substitute behavior to continue the same pattern of addiction, the same pattern of (emotional) avoidance.

If we continue to treat only the symptoms (addictive behaviors), no one will ever be cured. When we fail to address the force that drove a person to become an addict, we can never go beyond the behavior and find the underlying cause that continues to power the addiction train no matter what. This might be a depressing thought to someone who imagines that giving up one more thing represents losing only one more "pleasure." But take heart, once we face the reality of only one addiction, we get to give up the illusion that addressing only symptoms can heal it. Then, and only then, is a real cure possible.

CHAPTER ONE

A DISEASE OF DENIAL

I have absolutely no pleasure in the stimulants in which I sometimes so madly indulge. … It has been the desperate attempt to escape from torturing memories, … insupportable loneliness and a dread of some strange impending doom.
—Edgar Allan Poe

Substance abuse alone costs our nation more than $600 billion annually,[14] even though the public, as well as many mental health professionals, still fail to understand what addiction looks like. Abuse of tobacco, alcohol, and illicit drugs costs us more than $740 billion annually related to crime, lost work productivity, and health care.[15] Rampant denial has been fueled by society's willingness to keep normalizing bizarre behavior by promoting the illusory idea that the key to happiness is more of what ails you. Advertisers

---

[14] National Institute on Drug Abuse, "Contents," *Principles of Drug Addiction Treatment: A Research-Based Guide,* (third edition), updated January 2018, www.drugabuse.gov/publications/principles-drug-addiction-treatment-research-based-guide-third-edition/frequently-asked-questions/drug-addiction-treatment-worth-its-cost.

[15] National Institute on Drug Abuse, "Trends & Statistics," updated April 2017, www.drugabuse.gov/related-topics/trends-statistics.

trade on the idea that if you're not happy, you just need more unhealthy food, more medication, more money, more sex, more, more, more. So many of us have become affected that addiction has yet to be universally recognized as a progressive disease. Many people have a stereotyped image of an addict as someone in the throes of extreme behavior—broke, staggering, homeless, or institutionalized. Not true. Most of the addicts with whom I have worked are high-functioning members of society, that is, until they discover that they can no longer "manage" their addiction when they hit an emotional bottom, lose a relationship, or fail at a lucrative career and go broke. The famous and wealthy people with whom I have worked have had to hit an emotional bottom before they became ready to change. Money provides more distractions and a higher likelihood of veering off of a recovery course. When you consider all the ways that money and fame can enable one to pursue multiple addictions, it can be hard to break through the denial. I believe this is why so many celebrities wind up overdosing or committing suicide; they have become their own worst enemies, unable to keep a commitment to healing without introducing another distraction.

Denial is a failure to see how addictive behavior is different from "normal" behavior. For example, normal drinkers actually can start and stop at will; therefore, they do not experience multiple hangovers, blackouts, or any of the other signs of a problem drinker. Normal drinkers are satisfied with a drink or two and often leave some of the beverage unconsumed. Since most alcoholics hang with other alcoholics, their peers may all agree about what's "normal," but people who don't have problems with alcohol, don't have these symptoms. Normal drinkers are shocked by an incident when they experience any one of these symptoms and either make sure they never exceed their limit again or stop drinking entirely. Budding alcoholics will try all kinds of tricks to avoid these symptoms, but the fact of the matter is that they have already fallen into the maze of trying to *control*, and at that point, they're already in the maze, even though they don't know it yet. You might think that I'm overgeneralizing or being unrealistic. If so, I'd like to ask one simple question: If every time you ate an apple, you got sick, would you keep eating them? Of course not. Apples aren't addictive.

Addiction is not limited to drugs and alcohol. One thing all expressions of addiction have in common is that the symptoms grow worse over time. A food addict may gain only ten pounds a year, but in ten years, that's 100 pounds. A sex addict may occasionally masturbate to ease an urge when no partner is available, but over time, winds up masturbating to the point of physical injury, such as Peyronie's disease. A gambler may start off having fun at a poker table, but eventually will lose all possessions to the addiction.

No matter the form, addiction impacts everyone, and the longer the denial goes on, the worse the consequences become. A recent patient of mine, upon the death of her husband, had a rude awakening when she had to face the realities of his secret life. He had been found dead of a cocaine overdose, reported by his sex partner—a paid prostitute. Upon investigation, it was discovered that he had spent all the couple's money on drugs, illicit sex, and gambling. It will take many years for this patient to put the shattered pieces of her life back together.

The reason addiction isn't detected before dire consequences occur is most people are in denial about the symptoms. Short-term, denial isn't always a bad thing; it can protect us from an overload of shock, but sometimes we've been shocked repeatedly over a long stretch of time, and we don't ever come out of denial.

The denial of addiction is so subtle it doesn't allow the addicted person to see the truth. A person becomes so dependent on taking a substance or engaging in an activity in order to feel good that they lose touch with all of the things that provide lasting fulfillment. Addiction literally hijacks the rational part of the brain that fosters self-preservation and inserts the thought that you can't be happy without your vice. If anyone tries to address the behavior, addicted people respond with anger, a cover-up for the fear of losing their pacifier.

I recently spoke with a woman who had completed treatment for alcoholism. She was not at all happy with her recovery; she "missed her wine." When I explored her history further, she told me that prior to her excessive drinking she'd had gastric bypass surgery (abdominal resecting that reduces the ability to eat even normal quantities), a drastic measure for weight loss. No longer able to consume as much food or the kinds of food she preferred, she replaced her old favorite pastime with alcohol. It didn't take long for her to start drinking in the same way she'd been eating—around the clock. After treatment, she could indulge in neither, leaving her miserable. Like so many others who don't understand addiction, she didn't realize that she hadn't cured her addiction to food by having surgery. She had merely substituted alcohol for food.

How does this happen? Very easily. Here's an outline of a typical scenario, so you can see if any of this seems familiar to you. You try something, and it provides a feeling you've been missing: comfort, excitement, being accepted, pleasure. You like that feeling, so you keep doing the thing that provides the desired sensations. One day it hits you that things have gotten out of control, and you've gained too much weight, you've spent too much money, you've had one too many hangovers.

You take matters into your own hands and decide to do something about it. You muster up all of your willpower and you decide to quit. You make up your mind, you set a target date; it might get forwarded a few times, but eventually you stop. It's a little rough at first, but you like feeling back in control, you're losing weight, not missing work from too much partying, your finances improve, and you feel relieved. But after a period of time (may be short or long), it seems you're getting a whisper in your ear that, *It's been a long time; you've regained control, so it's OK to re-indulge just a little. After all, you're not supposed to be perfect, and you deserve a little treat for how "good" you've been. Not only that, but life has been pretty boring lately, and it's time to do something enjoyable, and since you now have control, you can fudge just a little, and everything will be fine. It's only for one occasion, and you'll get right back on track.*

And then when you sink your teeth into that first piece of creamy chocolate frosted cake, or have that first glass of your favorite wine, or you feel the thrill of risky living, it's almost as good as the first time. It's so good you can't wait to do it again; the promise of doing it only *one* time has vanished from your mind. The cycle of on and off continues ad infinitum, until you finally give up all together and don't even try to stop. At this point, your mind has been taken over by your addiction.

Addiction is similar to being slowly killed with rat poison; too often, by the time the symptoms appear, a person is so deep into the maze they can't get out. Alcoholics Anonymous warns that most untreated alcoholics wind up insane or dead. The insanity can be literal due to brain damage or due to loss of judgment, drinking while driving, missing work or performing work poorly, and/or all of the other insane behaviors of addiction in spite of all of the negative outcomes, including accidental death, death from poor health, and suicide.

The user rationalizes the symptoms to the point that health, mental soundness, or both become so severely impaired that they can no longer deny the problem exists. Unfortunately, many don't acknowledge the problem until the physical consequences (brain damage, bad health, insanity) become irreversible or the addict has lost everything of material or emotional importance.

The addict isn't the only one living in denial. There's usually a person in the addict's life who enables the addict. Enablers, often referred to as codependents, are addicted to the addict and demonstrate all the same signs and symptoms of addiction. The enabler could be an employer, a spouse, a friend, or a family member, anyone who unconsciously benefits from protecting the addict from the consequences of their choices. The codependent person relies on the addict in some way—emotionally, financially, or otherwise. Another scenario is when there is an unconscious collusion between two addicts: "I won't interfere with your addiction if you don't bug me about mine."

To illustrate what codependency looks like, here's a recap of a conversation I witnessed between an addiction counselor and the codependent girlfriend of a patient.

Girlfriend: I don't understand why you told my boyfriend that he needed to go to A.A.

Therapist: You're the one who told me he was driving drunk, and his personality had changed drastically. You also told me that when he drinks, he can't stop. When I gave him an evaluation, he had quite a few symptoms.

Girlfriend: Yes, but that was only a few occasions.

Therapist: You told me when he drinks, he loses control and his personality changes, and you fight.

Girlfriend: But that's why he never drinks.

Therapist: But then he does drink again in spite of the negative consequences.

Girlfriend: I just think you're judging him; I don't agree.

Therapist: I'm not judging him. I'm recognizing signs and symptoms of an illness. Just like any illness, it's best to diagnose it early.

Girlfriend: Well, I don't agree that he has signs of alcoholism; he just screwed up a few times.

Therapist: Tell me again why you broke up with him?

Girlfriend: Because he had issues, but I think it was his parents who screwed him up; they were definitely big drinkers.

Clearly, the patient's girlfriend was in denial, and her refusal to even consider that her ex-boyfriend might have symptoms of alcoholism enabled him to continue his self-destructive patterns instead of getting help. This is not only damaging to the addict, but it's dangerous for the codependent too, as they will often experience the same, or worse, impacts as the addict. This is why it's vital that we (and by "we," I mean therapists and laypeople) recognize the signs and symptoms, so we can intervene before it's too late. We don't have to wait until a person has completely lost their mind or life before we recognize a person has an addiction illness.

CHAPTER TWO

THE DIAGNOSIS DELUSION

For me, it is far better to grasp the Universe as it really is than to persist in delusion, however satisfying and reassuring.

—Carl Sagan

The current models for addiction diagnosis and treatment have failed to provide an adequate solution to help those who are addicted and often end up thwarting a person's chances of full recovery. As you're about to see, diagnosis criteria are inconsistent from one professional body to another, and none provides a comprehensive view. This greatly reduces the chances that a person suffering with an addiction will be properly diagnosed and receive the necessary treatment so they can heal.

I wish there were one perfect diagnostic model, but there's not. Each method of diagnosis has its shortcomings, the most common being a failure to recognize that all the various addictive behaviors are symptoms of one addiction.

The American Psychiatric Association defines addiction as "a brain *disease* exemplified by the compulsive use of substances in spite of negative consequences."[16] This diagnosis is limited to substances and excludes the hundreds of other compulsive behaviors that, when repeated, cause people to suffer horrific consequences.

The American Psychological Association (APA) refers to addiction as a chronic brain *disorder* that is influenced by biological, environmental, and psychological factors.[17] The APA views addiction as the voluntary use of mood-altering substances that, over time, become dependencies. This view does not explain the demise of people who become addicted involuntarily, like those who sustain traumatic injuries and, while unconscious, are given highly addictive narcotics such as morphine and Dilaudid, and awake to find themselves chemically dependent before they realize what has happened.

The Society of Addiction Psychology (Division 50 of the American Psychological Association) has recognized multiple addictive behaviors that include a wide range of compulsions beyond substance abuse, such as gambling, eating, sexual behavior, and spending.[18] Again, this diagnosis is limited to the same short list of behaviors as the other organizations, even though millions of people engaging in a myriad of other behaviors suffer the exact same symptoms. Even though each of the above organizations defines addiction in its own way, most mental health professionals refer to *The Diagnostic and Statistical Manual of Mental Disorders* (DSM) or the

---

[16] "What Is Addiction?" American Psychiatry Association, www.psychiatry.org/patients-families/addiction/what-is-addiction.

[17] "Addictions," American Psychological Association, www.apa.org/topics/addiction/.

[18] "Society of Addiction Psychology," American Psychological Association, www.apa.org/about/division/div50.

International Statistical Classification of Diseases and Related Health Problems (ICD) as their primary guide for diagnosis as well as treatment recommendations. The DSM recognizes just two kinds of "addiction," although the manual does not call it that; instead, it describes "substance use and gambling *disorders.*" Symptoms for substance disorders include abusing alcohol, cannabis, hallucinogens, opioids, sedatives, stimulants, and tobacco. Symptoms of gambling and substance-use "disorders" are: unsuccessful attempts to control how much and for how long substances are used, continued use in spite of negative consequences, psychological and/or physical withdrawal, and preoccupation with activities that involve either use or abuse activity. Both manuals avoid the word "addiction," and neither one extends the diagnosis to other behaviors with the same symptoms.

In 2011, the American Society of Addiction Medicine (ASAM) redefined addiction as "a disease of brain reward, motivation, memory, and related circuitry,"[19] and made it applicable to mood-altering substances and "other behaviors" that manifested in inconsistent abstinence, craving, loss of control, and emotional and interpersonal problems. ASAM also points out that several factors can trigger the addictive response. Even if the drug of choice is not within reach, any stimulus associated with using it (an ad, a memory, a smell, etc.) can trigger the craving. This phenomenon was demonstrated by the researcher Ivan Pavlov, who rang a bell every time he fed a group of dogs. After a few trials, the dogs salivated every time they heard a bell ring, regardless of whether or not food was

---

[19] American Society of Addiction Medicine, www.asam.org.

present. ASAM took a big step for mankind by recognizing "other behaviors," but they haven't yet taken the giant leap that it's all "one addiction."

Alcoholics Anonymous provides a self-diagnostic questionnaire[20] that pinpoints symptoms: failed attempts at stopping or limiting amounts of consumption, switching from one type of alcohol to another, morning drinking, problems related to drinking, missed work, and blackouts. The symptoms listed are congruent with the aforementioned criteria, but without an addiction professional, someone who has an alcohol problem might look at these questions and say, "So what? Doesn't everyone have these symptoms every once in a while?"

Actually, no.

Although not used as often as the above sources, there are better evaluation techniques for diagnosing addiction. My favorite is the Jellinek Curve. Developed by E. M. Jellinek in the 1950s, the Jellinek Curve charts the progressive symptoms and phases of alcoholism, but I find the chart applicable to any addiction. Jellinek refers to the "early-stage alcoholic," who uses alcohol to feel better, relieve anxiety, escape emotional pain, and who, over time, experiences memory loss, keeps a stash, and increases dependency, with ever-increasing consequences. The "middle-stage" symptoms are reproof by family and friends, failed attempts to control usage, violation of one's own moral standards, missed work, blackouts and health problems, and increased tolerance for the substance. The "chronic-stage"

---

[20] "Is A.A. for You?" Alcoholic Anonymous, www.aa.org/pages/en_US/is-aa-for-you-twelve-questions-only-you-can-answer.

includes an obsession with alcohol, withdrawal, delirium, tremors, alcohol psychosis, impaired thinking, and failed health. I like to use this chart because it identifies the early signs and symptoms—before the addiction has become all-consuming and the person's life rotates around the addiction. Like any illness, the sooner the diagnosis, the better the prognosis. When using this chart, I often visualize the mouse in the maze, moving from one corridor to the next, becoming ever more lost as it wanders and loses its ability to find its way out.

The Jellinek chart also shows the progression out of the addiction and into recovery from the desire for help and stopping the behavior to finding a support system, self-care, therapy, and so on. I feel the Jellinek chart is the best diagnostic technique, because it provides a comprehensive map that can be used to guide the patient and the diagnostician to track the progressive symptoms of addiction and the recovery process in an accurate and specific manner that is applicable to all forms of addiction. However, it does not address cross-addiction or the underlying cause, and it should be seen as a useful process in early-stage recovery and be followed with an emphasis on addressing the wounds that precipitated the addiction in the first place.

When we put all of these diagnostic criteria together, we get a mishmash of similarities and differences. The scope of what constitutes an addiction varies greatly. While there is some consensus on signs and symptoms, some won't even use the word "addiction." Nor is there agreement that the symptoms cited would apply to *any* addiction, or the fact that all addictions are the same, and if a person has one and gives it up, they are likely to substitute something else unless and until the root cause is addressed.

Where All Diagnoses Miss the Mark

Most problematic is that in every case, the addictive behavior is seen as the *source* of the problem rather than the symptom of an underlying cause. This is at the crux of why so many people fail to get diagnosed and why, even when the diagnosis is accurate and a particular compulsive behavior stops, the addiction rarely ends. Treatments that are considered "successful" often mean that the patient has simply switched from one addictive behavior to another.

During the thirty years I've spent in my practice as of this writing, I've seen multiple examples of misdiagnosis and the subsequent consequences. Three classic ones that I see most frequently are: mistaking grief and trauma for a mood disorder, such as anxiety or depression, or misperceiving an existing addiction as a mood disorder and prescribing narcotics to someone who is in recovery, and failing to recognize the probability of relapse into another form. The following cases describe each of these three common errors clinicians make.

One example of mistaking addiction as a mood disorder occurred with a patient of mine whom I'll call Mary, who as a child had been sexually abused and verbally berated by her father. She was prescribed Valium for her panic attacks. Her physician never asked her why she was anxious or explored the source of her anxiety, but he did make sure to tell her,

"This is a chemical imbalance in your body, and your anxiety will never go away." When a physician so adamantly and authoritatively makes such a declaration, it tends to become a fixed thought in a person's mind—especially an addict's mind. The addict hears what the addict wants to hear: "Drugs are good for you."

It's bad enough that this patient was abused as a child, but it was even worse that a doctor told her she could wipe away all the pain of that abuse with a magic pill. The message here: "It's not OK to be upset with the fact that your own parent violated your trust, took advantage of you, and left a wound on you that you would carry for the rest of your life." I'm not sure which form of abuse is worse.

Over the next twenty years, the patient cycled between alcohol and Valium with an ever-increasing dependence on both. She was scared to stop taking the medication because she'd been told that medication was the only treatment for her anxiety. Exploring the root cause, as we did, had never been presented to her as an alternative. She had spent most of her life numbed out on substances, yet she had grown tired of being medicated, so she sought therapy and mustered up the courage to investigate the cause of her addiction, so she could let go of drugs and discover her real self.

Mary's case presents an example of mistaking an unresolved trauma for a mood disorder which led to addiction. Mary had gone to a psychiatrist for depression because she was sad most of the time. She didn't have the energy to do anything, and her interest in family and friends had diminished to almost nothing. She told the therapist she had been in treatment years before for cocaine, but no one had told her to stay away from all mood-altering substances. No one warned her that her brain wouldn't know the difference. No one asked or realized that, even though she had stopped using illicit drugs, she continued to drink alcohol.

The psychiatrist had prescribed an antidepressant, but when she didn't improve, she was referred to a psychotherapist, and after years of counseling, she remained depressed. All the while she'd been drinking alcohol every night in increasing amounts to the point that her antidepressant medication stopped working. When Mary was referred to me, she was shocked to hear my suggestion that if she were not saturating her brain with a depressive drug every night, she might be able to benefit from therapy. She had never been shown the connection between her persistent sense of depression and the fact that she was consuming large amounts of alcohol and Valium (both of which are depressive drugs) every day.

Bob, who was in recovery then was prescribed narcotics, exemplifies the second common misstep by therapists. Bob went to a psychiatrist because he was suffering from anxiety. He'd been sober for a year, and he couldn't sleep. His mind was spinning. A physical exam provided him a clean bill of health. The psychiatrist told him he was suffering from anxiety and prescribed Valium, which produces the same effect as having a drink, and Ambien for sleep, another mood-altering drug that is unsafe for recovering addicts. Bob found himself taking the Valium every couple of hours during the night because he liked the effect of feeling high. When his anxiety did not subside, his psychiatrist told him he needed psychotherapy. His new therapist, not an addiction counselor, failed to see that Bob was in relapse. Bob liked having someone to talk to, so he continued therapy even though he wasn't getting better. The only thing he accomplished was relapsing and adding three new pieces of cheese (Valium, Ambien, and therapy) to keep him running in his maze.

To illustrate the third example, take Raymond. On the verge of relapsing with drugs and alcohol, Raymond decided he needed help. He'd already been to therapy because, after two years of sobriety, he felt worse than when he was drinking. He'd spent his whole life using a bottle to nurse his emotional wounds, and now that he'd put it down, he could barely tolerate his emotional ups and downs. Recovery meetings weren't enough. He understood that he could no longer use any type of mood-altering drug, but as he got sober, he started eating excessive amounts of chocolate to "soothe" himself, especially at night, which had been his favorite time to drink and do drugs. Around the same time, Raymond developed a crush on another A.A. member he had started dating—obsessively. When he wasn't seeing his lover, his thoughts would fixate on her. He'd wonder what she was doing and who she was with, obsessing about her as if she were a drug, going through withdrawal (anxiety and sleepless nights) when he could not see her, becoming angry and agitated when he couldn't have sex on demand with her, and missing work to be with her.

While it might seem that Raymond had "overcome" his addiction to drugs and alcohol, his new fixations showed that he had merely transferred his addiction from drugs and alcohol to chocolate, romance, and sex—all producing the same high. A layperson might think this isn't such a bad trade-off, but Raymond was left with nagging cravings that made him feel like a caged, starving lion looking for his next meal. He was not feeling "grateful" for his sobriety. He still wanted to drink. At least with alcohol and drugs, he was able to keep himself comfortably numb.

Raymond was still in the maze. He had not recovered from addiction. He merely switched to a new brand of cheese. He did not realize it was all the same addiction, and he would have to heal the underlying cause or continue to be driven by his yearnings.

All of these examples are real-life situations. I've witnessed situations similar to Raymond's many times, including in my own life. Starting at age fifteen, I'd been to numerous psychologists, all of whom failed to diagnose my own addiction or see how addiction had destroyed my childhood and two marriages. Later, when I began my career as a mental health counselor, I realized the inadequacies of my professional training. Even though I'd interned in two mental health facilities, by the time I'd received my master's degree in psychology and worked in private practice, I'd had little training in mental illness or addictions. Yet when I asked patients about habits with which they were concerned, I realized almost everyone I was treating either had been raised in a family with addiction, had an addiction, or was involved with an addict. Lacking the right skills to diagnose and treat these individuals, I took a proactive stance and read, attended continuing education classes, went to recovery meetings, and consulted with treatment centers.

Having personally gone to five therapists (over a ten-year period), none of whom had recognized addiction in my family or in me, I came to see that there was a competency gap among mental health providers in my community. As a result, when I did my doctoral dissertation, I developed a training program on chemical dependency for nurses and mental health professionals at Palm Beach Community College (now Palm Beach State College) in Lake Worth, Florida, so they could get continuing education credits, learn about the signs and symptoms of addiction, and make appropriate referrals.

When I started to quantify the need for this type of community education, I set out to measure their level of knowledge about the signs and symptoms of alcoholism. The quiz had twenty questions, all of which presented the signs and symptoms of alcoholism. The results were shocking. Only one person scored above 70 percent.

Through a collaborative effort between Donna DiSessa, the college's continuing education director; Robert Bozzone, the executive director at Comprehensive Alcohol and Rehabilitation Program (CARP); and myself, we implemented the program in 1990. As of this writing, that program has evolved into a comprehensive addiction studies program offering college credit and meeting the requirements for the Florida Certification Board for addiction.[21]

---

[21] "Human Services," Palm Beach State College, palmbeachstate.edu/programs/humanservices/default.aspx.

Redefining Addiction

Proper diagnosis is the key to the cure. People can't get well if their condition is not correctly defined. The addicted person cannot recover if the very people treating them don't understand the problem. Just like it would be intolerable if doctors consistently diagnosed cancer as heart disease, we need to start calling out addiction for what it is—persistent and deadly. A person can become addicted to *anything*: alcohol, drugs, exercise, food, gambling, another person, nicotine, vaping, prescription narcotics, religion, shopping, self-help programs, sex, power, video games, work, and the list goes on. Addicts all are searching for the same thing—a moment of euphoria. Whether it's the cigarette smoker with lung cancer who keeps smoking, the workaholic with chronic chest pains on the verge of a massive coronary, or the guy who's headed for divorce because his wife keeps walking in on him while he's on a porn site, they all share the same symptoms. Each of these examples puts the person in the position of behaving like a mouse in a maze looking for cheese.

Even worse, rather than science helping people get free of addiction, science is helping people find new and better ways to stay addicted. For example, e-cigarettes keep the smoker hooked on nicotine without having to stop the habit. Naltrexone allows alcoholics and addicts to keep using without getting the same high. Pills allow people to keep temporarily calm without discovering the source of their anxiety. All of these solutions deliver the message to stay addicted. Rather than helping addicts get out of the maze, the medical world has joined them.

The current death rate from addictive behaviors (mostly alcohol, drugs, food, and smoking) is staggering. According to the World Health Organization, 3.3 million die annually from alcohol abuse,[22] 130 people a day (47,450 annually) die from opioid overdose,[23] and obesity and being overweight are the second leading cause of preventable deaths (300,000 annually).[24] There are 480,000 deaths per year from conditions related to cigarette smoking.[25] In 2017, 70,237 drug overdose deaths were reported,[26] and according to the Centers for Disease Control and Prevention, 15,482 deaths were related to heroin overdose that same year.[27] Every fifteen minutes, a baby is born suffering from opioid withdrawal.[28] This is crazy! Continuing to misrepresent these deadly conditions as "disorders" is not only irresponsible, but it fails to induce clear and early intervention.

What's it going to take for us to wake up?

Clearly, addiction does not operate in the fashion that the medical and psychological communities have defined. I invite you to consider a better definition: **Addiction is *anything* a**

[22] World Health Organization, "Alcohol," *Management of Substance Abuse*, www.who.int/substance_abuse/facts/alcohol/en/.
[23] National Institute on Drug Abuse, "Overdose Death Rates," revised January 2019, www.drugabuse.gov/related-topics/trends-statistics/overdose-death-rates.
[24] West Virginia Department of Health and Human Resources, "Obesity: Facts, Figures, and Guidelines," December 2002, www.wvdhhr.org/bph/oehp/obesity/mortality.htm.
[25] Centers for Disease Control and Prevention, "Diseases and Death," last reviewed February 6, 2019, www.cdc.gov/tobacco/data_statistics/fact_sheets/fast_facts/index.htm.
[26] "Overdose Death Rates," www.cdc.gov/drugoverdose/data/statedeaths.html
[27] Ibid.
[28] Christina Echegaray, "Early Discharge of NAS Infants Prolongs Treatment," Vanderbilt University Medical Center, September 25, 2018, www.vumc.org/childhealthpolicy/news-events/early-discharge-nas-infants-prolongs-treatment.

person keeps doing regardless of adverse or painful consequences.

This definition might seem oversimplified, but no rational, non-addicted person continues to do anything at the expense of personal health or financial security or risks the loss of family and friends. An addicted person has lost the ability to stop and *stay stopped*. Examples include: the alcoholic who keeps drinking in spite of numerous DUIs and illnesses; the gambler who gets in debt then borrows and steals to cover bets; the drug addict who keeps increasing the dose until they overdose; the opioid addict who remains on massive amounts of pain medication years after an injury; the food addict who is now obese, diabetic, and on the verge of a massive heart attack yet continues to eat in a way that exacerbates this illness. These are only a few examples of people who may think they are in control, but really they are addicts in the maze.

They may even *temporarily* stop, but it doesn't take long for the thoughts, *I can have just a little. This time it will be different*, to draw the addict deeper into the maze. Because as long as the addict is using willpower to stay away from the addiction, the battle will become so exhausting that eventually the addict is bound to give in.

By the time Sherry came to see me, she'd lost everything. She was extremely thin, middle-aged, and gaunt. She'd started as an occasional drinker: a couple of drinks socially, then every weekend, and then every night, with her starting time moving up earlier and earlier. The more she drank, the more she needed to drink to escape the consequences of her drinking. Even after she'd been arrested for driving under the influence, she'd stay in bed in the morning, neglecting to properly care for her two children and unable to hold down a job. She swore off drinking many times but always found herself in a bar with friends, as she journeyed further into the maze.

Her husband said he would file for divorce and take custody of the kids if Sherry came home drunk again. She went to see a therapist who put her on an antidepressant, and she was able to stay sober for a couple of weeks, but one night while out to dinner with a friend, she forgot the warning and ordered a glass of wine. For the umpteenth time, she told herself that since she'd been sober for a couple of weeks, she could handle having one drink. Within minutes, once the alcohol hit her brain, she forgot all about the pain and suffering alcohol had brought her. She staggered home at three o'clock in the morning; by the time she got home, all the locks had been changed, and she had to sleep in her car.

When she awoke, her family was gone, and she had to stay with a relative. Three months later, she was divorced with no money, no family, no career, no life, and still she continued to drink. In spite of losing everything dear to her, she had deluded herself into thinking that her husband and kids left because they didn't love her, even though her now ex-husband had told her he still would help her if she sobered up. She continued to try to control her drinking and continued to fail. She could not accept the fact that she was powerless to moderate her drinking, and that whenever she had that first drink, she would be unable to predict what would happen, how much she would consume, where she would wake up, or what she would say or do.

Sherry's former husband attended her second therapy session and pleaded with her to get sober. He told her the children needed her, and he needed her, too. She broke into tears and said she "couldn't." My heart broke for this family. Sherry was so far along in the addiction, it seemed there was too much brain damage, and she'd lost her ability to reason. Sherry never returned to therapy, though her husband came in for a few sessions in an attempt to understand her actions and to grieve.

Other than the preferred brand of "cheese," the alcoholic who continues to drink is no different than the excitement junkie who continues to shoplift items they can afford to purchase, despite the public shame and humiliation of being caught, or the sex addict who is arrested for soliciting prostitutes and goes for another prostitute the next week, or the food addict who eats to the point of life-threatening illness.

Though it may take years, once a person develops the habit of denial and repetition compulsion, this individual succumbs to the mental obsession. Just the thought of getting the fix triggers the dopamine receptors in the brain and the chase is on. Just as Pavlov described with his salivating dogs and the sound of the bell, anything that activates the mental image sets the addiction wheels into motion. It is like falling into a deep hole without a rope; when you try to get out, you make a little progress as you dig your fingers and toes into the side of the dirt wall, only to slide back down every time. Other people can see the person spinning more and more out of control, but the person who is addicted is too far into the maze to see reality—or even want to.

One study by James Olds and Peter Milner demonstrates the power of the pleasure center in the brain.[29] Rats' brains were implanted with electrodes in the septal area just above the hypothalamus, the brain's reward center. The electrodes stimulated the hypothalamus every time the rat pushed a lever. The rats compulsively pushed the lever, up to thousands of times per hour, to the point that they would refuse to eat, avoid sex, abandon their young, run across electrical shock, or do anything to get another "hit." The researchers finally had to end the experiment before the rats died of starvation.[30] People who are addicted exhibit the same type of behavior; they will push the limits to the extreme, risking everything they value in order to get the reward, even if it means losing it all, including their own lives.

This leads me to the biggest problem of all: Even when a person gives up one addictive pattern, they usually find another to take its place. I have yet to work with someone in recovery whose addiction didn't (unknowingly) transfer to another form (i.e., the addict who stops drugging and starts drinking, the recovering smoker who switches to sugar, the recovering alcoholic who switches to love or sex addiction).

All addictions follow the same diagnostic criteria of being powerless to control their addiction—permanently. Like any illness, it can be cured, but it can't reverse itself. Once the

---

[29] James Olds and Peter Milner. "Positive Reinforcement Produced by Electrical Stimulation of Septal Area and Other Regions of Rat Brain," *Journal of Comparative and Physiological Psychology*, 47 no. 6 (1954): 419-427, dx.doi.org/10.1037/h0058775.
[30] David J. Linden, "The Neuroscience of Pleasure," *Huffpost: The Blog*, July 7, 2011, updated September 6, 2011, www.huffpost.com/entry/compass-pleasure_b_890342.

person has become addicted, there is no reversing the control factor. An alcoholic will never learn how to drink alcohol moderately. A gambler will never bet controlled amounts. A food addict will never control the intake of foods to which they are addicted. While it is normal for most addicts to relapse, the focus must be on recovery and healing. Only with abstinence can a person get enough distance from the behavior to begin to understand that any manifestation of addiction must be replaced with genuine self-love, or the drive to use another way to get "high" will remain.

If all this sounds discouraging, take heart. By the time you finish reading this book, you may see your addiction as a blessing in disguise. You may come to realize that addiction has a purpose. It presents an opportunity to heal something much deeper, and if you do the work, it can lead you on a path to genuine self-love.

Pretty soon, I'm going to show you how you can find your way out of the maze and be free of addiction once and for all. But first, I'm going to share with you how we need to rethink treatment, so not only can you see there is a solution, but you'll also get a good sense of how you can achieve it. I'll give you a map out of the maze.

Self-Evaluation Questionnaire

1. Have you ever felt you have tried to control something but were unsuccessful? Describe those situations.

2. When you were unsuccessful, describe what happened.

3. Have you ever been in counseling to try to control a particular behavior? If so, what?

4. Were you successful? Why or why not?

5. If you have tried to stop doing something multiple times, have you given up on trying?

6. Write down a time in your life you felt stuck at something.

7. Describe someone you know who has an addiction. If you knew the person before they became addicted, did you see warning signs? If so, describe them.

CHAPTER THREE

THE TREATMENT TRAP

I have not failed. I've just found 10,000 ways that won't work.

—Thomas Edison

The current models for treating addiction rely on ineffective strategies that add up to the equivalent of trying to teach a mouse to stop pushing the lever that dispenses the morphine. The reason is that the most utilized treatment strategies focus on stopping the addiction (the symptom), not healing the cause.

Abstinence will stop the behavior but not the addiction. In fact, all willful attempts to stop or reduce the addictive behavior only intensify the obsession. Studies have shown that for heavy drinkers, parts of the brain that can help control a drinking habit are damaged, which makes the pursuit of moderation not just a matter of will but a physical impossibility.[31]

Please note that any reference I make to treatment for substances applies to all flavors of addiction because they are

---

[31] Christopher Wanjek, "Controlled Drinking: Controversial Alternative to A.A.," *LiveScience*, December 4, 2007, www.livescience.com/2065-controlled-drinking-controversial-alternative-aa.html.

all expressions of the same disease, which I will explain later. The treatment models are pretty much the same also—you give up the thing to which you are addicted. There are exceptions. Obviously, for food, you would abstain from the foods you are addicted to—usually wheat and sugar—and learn to eat healthily. For sex, you would abstain from harmful sexual behaviors and replace those with healthy sexual intimacy. I'd also like to note that even though not all compulsive behaviors have to be medically detoxed, all do have components of emotional and physical withdrawal—the jonesing effect that shows up across any manifestation of addiction—and is always painful.

Medication

The medical community has three ways they use medications to treat addictions: detox, psychiatric medications, and harm reduction.

Detox: Hospitals, mental health facilities, and detox centers are available for detoxification from excessive amounts of alcohol or drugs. "Getting clean" is the first step of the recovery process, though not every patient intends to stop using; some just want to "dry out." Detox typically occurs in a confined setting; however, some outpatient clinics will detox patients if they have a proper caregiver at home to administer meds and watch the patient carefully. One of the disadvantages of this approach is that the recovering person does not connect with other people in detox or treatment and remains isolated, thus being less likely to attend recovery meetings and make new friends.

There are several medications prescribed for detoxification. Benzodiazepines (sedatives) and anticonvulsants are administered to reduce withdrawal symptoms and the chance of seizures. Benzodiazepines can cause severe depression, psychosis, and suicidal ideology, and can be deadly when mixed with alcohol.[32] Naltrexone blocks the euphoric effect of opiates and reduces cravings during withdrawal. Suboxone and methadone are used to treat withdrawal from opioids, but both are highly addictive. All detox drugs are prescribed on a temporary basis to help the addict wean off the drug to which they are addicted.

One problem with detox is that many programs do not provide the therapy necessary for long-term remission. Many patients use detox centers to medically withdraw then start drinking or drugging again. A physician at a local hospital recently referred a patient to me who had detoxed five times within a few months. When I met with the patient, it was clear she had no intention of doing the work necessary to stay sober, especially since she was able to use the hospital as her legal drug dealer. When she couldn't stop drinking, the patient would get detoxed on massive doses of benzodiazepines then go on to stay sober for a week or two and repeat the patterns all over again. She simply used the detox medication to get high while she wasn't drinking.

I believe that detox centers could expand to address all manifestations of addiction. Since withdrawal from any addictive behavior has the same symptoms of anger, irritability,

---

[32] Peter R. Breggin, "Brain-Disabling Effects of Benzodiazepines," *Brain-Disabling Treatments in Psychiatry*, www.benzo.org.uk/breggin.htm.

depression, and craving, a one- or two-week stay in a facility could ease the withdrawal. Temporary emotional support, safety, and self-care could stabilize a person, reduce chances of relapse, and prepare the person for intensive outpatient therapy and adequate support upon discharge—something that is currently lacking.

Prevention: Antabuse is a medication that is given to alcoholics after they are detoxed to prevent relapse. The patient is responsible for taking a pill that when mixed with alcohol causes nausea, dizziness, chest pain, and other unpleasant effects. It only works if taken daily, and once alcoholics decide to drink, they set the pill aside.

Psychiatric Medications: Some medications are necessary if a person has a secondary mood or mental disorder such as anxiety, depression, personality disorder, or psychotic disorder. On the other hand, someone in emotional or physical withdrawal might exhibit all of the symptoms of mental illness, but given some time for the brain to regulate, these symptoms often subside. It is my opinion that in the past twenty years, the trend has been to prematurely render a dual diagnosis because many insurance companies will provide additional benefits for mental disorders.

Antidepressants: In the 1980s and early 1990s, unless a patient was severely impaired, it was customary to wait a year before prescribing antidepressant medication. At that time, depression was classified under two categories. Reactive depression was due to an environmental stress such as loss of a loved one and was typically treated with therapy. The other type was a neurochemical imbalance, which was treated with medication. If the environmentally induced stress was severe, such as the unexpected loss of a spouse or a child or being the victim of a violent crime, short-term medication was sometimes prescribed to stabilize the patient enough for them to benefit from therapy.

In 1980, when the third revision of the *Diagnostic and Statistical Manual* was released, there was an attempt to "re-medicalize" American psychiatry.[33] The DSM-III elected to put all depressive and manic conditions under the category of "mood disorders,"[34] and this kicked off a slow shift toward prescribing more medication for these types of diagnoses. Now under the classification of mood disorders, depression due to environmental stress is regularly treated with medication, and in many cases, it is prescribed as an alternative to therapy. At the very least, a person should be given the opportunity to grieve a loss or process trauma before medicating the pain with an antidepressant.

These patients are prescribed serotonin reuptake inhibitors (SSRIs), which reduce symptoms by increasing serotonin levels in the brain. The most common drugs are Celexa, Lexapro, Paxil, Prozac, and Zoloft. These medications are not mood altering, but as I mentioned earlier, many patients who remain on these types of medications for a long period of time, then want to stop, go through a different kind of hell wrought with the symptoms of withdrawal experienced by any addict.

---

[33] Shadia Kawa and James Giordano, "A Brief Historicity of the *Diagnostic and Statistical Manual of Mental Disorders:* Issues and Implications for the Future of Psychiatric Canon and Practice," *PubMed Central,* January 13, 2012, www.ncbi.nlm.nih.gov/pmc/articles/PMC3282636/.

[34] Nancy McWilliams, *Psychoanalytic Diagnosis,* (New York, The Guilford Press, 2011).

One patient, Jill, struggled with an eating disorder and depression and had been on an antidepressant medication for ten years. At the time, she was not happy in her marriage, her husband traveled, and she often was left alone at home with their two children. When her husband was home, he showed little interest in her, and she used food to soothe herself. Her medical doctor told her she was suffering from "clinical depression" and prescribed an antidepressant. (Jill should have been referred to a psychotherapist first.) Two of the side effects of the medication were weight gain and decreased sexual interest including the inability to have orgasms. During her therapy, we discussed getting to the bottom of her pain, so she could heal the feelings underneath her depression. She felt that the medication had made her emotionally numb, and she wanted to go off of it, so she could "get herself back." Under her physician's care, she was slowly weaned off the medication over a six-month period during which Jill suffered bouts of severe anxiety, clamminess, insomnia, nightmares, obsessive thoughts, and morbid feelings in the morning, all symptoms she'd never experienced before taking antidepressants. It took over a year for Jill to begin to feel back to her old self, and she often said had she known about the side effects, she never would have started the medication.

Anti-Anxiety Medications: Anxiety can be treated with some of the same SSRIs as depression, but sometimes anxiety is treated with a benzodiazepine, such as Valium, Xanax, or Ativan, all mood-altering substances. Like other sedative drugs, they create a sense of calm or euphoria, and for someone prone to addiction, they aren't much different than drinking or drugging away the anxiety. Again, the anxiety should be treated with psychotherapy prior to medication whenever possible.

Antipsychotic Drugs: While it is critical that someone who genuinely suffers from a dual diagnosis be provided the necessary medication, I do feel this should not be made in haste. A psychiatrist can order bloodwork to determine a true chemical imbalance, and if warranted, this should be done at regular intervals to adjust the medication as necessary. Most antipsychotic drugs are not addictive.

A person who genuinely suffers a dual diagnosis (an addiction paired with a mental disorder) will need to be on medication to stabilize their mental disorder before they can benefit from addiction treatment. Secondary disorders are treated with medicine that is not mood altering but will regulate the chemical imbalance in the brain. Someone who has a mental disorder will need to be informed that it is critical they stay on the medication.

Medication has an important place in treating addiction and mental illness. It is miraculous that a person suffering from schizophrenia, bipolar disorder, or suicidal ideation can be given a non-mood-altering pill and be asymptomatic. Further, there is little chance of these people staying sober when they are suffering from psychosis (visual and auditory hallucinations, delusional thinking) without being stabilized first. My only concern is that often a patient is prematurely diagnosed with anxiety or depression, or even substance-induced psychosis, and once again, rather than helping a person work through what's causing their symptoms, the symptoms are medicated, which only keeps the person stuck in their pain rather than healing it. In any case, after detox, psychiatrists and physicians should never prescribe mood-altering drugs. The addict is prone to take any mood-altering medication offered, so prescribing it only expands the addict's repertoire of drugs. To an addict, a drug is a drug is a drug, and once the substance is in the brain, the cycle resumes wherever it left off. More cheese, please.

A final note about medication and children. Many teens in addiction treatment were put on Ritalin or Adderall as children. These drugs are stimulants used to treat psychiatric symptoms such as attention-deficit disorder, obsessive-compulsive disorder, sleep disorders, aggression, anxiety, depression, and bipolar disorder. Regardless of whether the medication works or not, some children become addicted.[35]

The trend of putting children on medications that could permanently alter their brain's natural ability to regulate itself is alarming indeed. Some researchers have warned about the adverse effects of medicating children and have indicated family therapy should be the recommended treatment.[36]

It seems foolhardy to me to mess with a kid's brain while it is still developing then expect it to be able to operate in a normal fashion. Kids who are hyper, compulsive, and depressed often are sent to school having eaten sugar-laden, processed

[35] The National Institute on Drug Abuse for Teens Blog Team, "Prescription Drugs," *Drugs & Health Blogs*, revised May 2019, www.teens.drugabuse.gov/drug-facts/prescription-drugs.
[36] Columbia University Medical Center, "Psychiatric Medications Are Not Overprescribed for Kids, Finds Study," *ScienceDaily*, January 29, 2018, www.sciencedaily.com/releases/2018/01/180129181419.htm.

foods (or nothing) for breakfast, are rushed to school by a stressed-out parent, or are exposed to trauma at school, home, or elsewhere—or all of the above. To put a child on medication without exhausting all other alternatives teaches the child the defect is in them and a pill will fix everything—the perfect formula for future addiction. Medicating a child should be used only as a last resort and only with the child's thorough understanding that it's a medical problem and not a personal defect.

Harm Reduction: Medically assisted treatment (MAT) is offered when a person fails at numerous attempts in treatment. Patients are prescribed drugs from which they are supposed to be titrated, along with counseling and attendance at recovery meetings. Methadone, Suboxone, and naltrexone are prescribed for opiate addiction. Women who are opiate addicts and pregnant are administered methadone to prevent mother and fetal withdrawal and buprenorphine to reduce cravings[37] for all opioids including morphine and heroin. Chantix is prescribed for smoking cessation and nicotine replacement therapy (NRT) is administered as an alternative to smoking. Naltrexone, which reduces the euphoric effects of alcohol, is also given to alcoholics so they can drink without craving more.

Huh? I'm not sure why giving up on a program of abstinence is a good idea. There is the assumption that it's just too hard for the addict to stop rather than looking more carefully at

---

[37] North Carolina Pregnancy & Opioid Exposure Project, "Medication-Assisted Treatment (MAT) in Pregnancy—Overview," www.ncpoep.org/guidance-document/north-carolina-guidelines-medication-assisted-treatment-mat-in-pregnancy/mat-in-pregnancy/.

the relapse triggers and responses. Giving additional dangerous drugs to people so they can better manage their drug use seems to be just another way to keep people addicted. Many MAT patients do not seek counseling or recovery meetings and are not weaned off of the drugs, another shortcoming of this program. This harm reduction method is based on the notion that addicts should be given drugs to reduce the negative consequences of using. Rather than trying to force abstinence or wean the addict, the drug abuser is provided the substances needed to prevent illicit drug use, overdose, spread of infectious diseases, and other harmful outcomes. Methadone is prescribed for heroin and other opiate addicts, and needle facilities are provided as well.

It is highly unlikely that many people under the harm reduction model voluntarily would seek help to stop an addiction. People in these programs are unlikely to recover because they are being given the subliminal message that they should *give up* trying to stop.

Another grave concern I have about MAT has come about recently. Several new patients have come to see me and reported that even though they'd been in A.A. and maintained sobriety for a long time, they are now smoking pot. They have reported they were effortlessly prescribed a license to receive medical marijuana and have surrendered their recovery to relapse on pot. One patient who was thinking about smoking it told me it was a "gray area," and he received clarification when I told him it was not a gray area; it's black and white. You're either sober or you're not.

The form of marijuana that was legally approved for genuine medical conditions such as pain control and reducing nausea from chemotherapy is supposed to have minimal amounts of THC, so that it is not mood altering. The dozens of people I've spoken with who are on today's brand of "medical marijuana" say, "It's the best pot I've ever had." Lots of people in A.A. are now smoking pot under the illusion they are sober. All of the people who have come to see me are in the throes of an emotional crash. They have suffered numerous consequences including having traumatized their children who had been proud of their parent's sobriety. It's clear to see that none of these people had been cured of their addiction in the first place or they would not have taken such risks.

My big beef with medically assisted treatment is that it's becoming compulsory, mandated by insurance companies that, for example, won't pay for treatment of drug addiction unless a patient is put on Suboxone. In some instances, employees of MAT facilities are going out into the community and recruiting potential patients, including the homeless, so they can pull more people into their programs and get more government funding. My belief is that MAT should be given as a last resort.

While it is important to respect a person's right to do what they want with their bodies, I'm not sure why providing legal drugs to a drug addict is considered treatment and not enabling. Giving drugs to addicts is just another way of lowering the bar and helping them use drugs rather than helping them to recover. Yes, it's certainly better for a person to be legally administered a controlled substance if it helps them lead a relatively functional life rather than winding up in jail, being homeless, or contracting a disease. Drug addiction treatment is much less expensive than its alternatives, such as incarcerating addicted persons, and treatment doesn't isolate the person from their family.[38] I also agree that it is good to eliminate all criminal elements of drug addiction, but if that's the route we're going to take, why not legalize all drugs, tax them, and use the funds for education and prevention? We could start with teaching parents to lead by example and teach their children it is never a good idea to poison their precious, lovable bodies and developing brains with deadly substances.

Treatment Centers/Rehab

Up until the mid-1900s, people suffering from alcoholism or drug addiction were sent to asylums, but once released from the hospital, patients usually relapsed. Though there aren't many records available tracking the length of time between sobering up and relapsing, we can gauge that it wasn't very long, as there were no preventive procedures available until A.A. came along.

When A.A. was founded, a recovering alcoholic would be called to the asylum or hospital to help the patient understand the addiction to alcohol, show them how to stop, and offer ongoing support of personal contact and meetings. Once

---

[38] National Institute on Drug Abuse, "Is Drug Addiction Treatment Worth Its Cost?" *Principles of Drug Addiction Treatment: A Research-Based Guide*, (third edition), updated January 2018, www.drugabuse.gov/publications/principles-drug-addiction-treatment-research-based-guide-third-edition/frequently-asked-questions/drug-addiction-treatment-worth-its-cost.

successful, the newly sober person would "pass it on" by helping others who were also suffering from alcoholism.

Over the past thirty years, treatment centers have become the go-to place for people who need help for an addiction. There are treatment centers for every possible addiction— most substances, food, gambling, sex, and codependency. *Market Watch* reported that there are more than 14,000 treatment centers in the United States, pulling in annual revenue of $35 billion.[39] Patients may go to treatment voluntarily, through a court order, or as a result of a family intervention. Many treatment centers follow A.A.'s 12-Step (or similar) model, including education about the signs and symptoms of addiction, evaluation for medication, counseling, exercise, meditation, family education, and aftercare. Treatment can be outpatient or inpatient and may range from thirty days up to a year or two. It is estimated that 40 to 60 percent of people who receive treatment will relapse.[40]

Many treatment centers are staffed with a team having varied amounts of training and differing views. On far too many occasions, staff have undermined progress or treatment plans with referrals, creating another "dysfunctional family" scenario: When a referring therapist sends a patient to treatment, a collaborative effort should be made to ensure the patient's safety and continuing treatment after discharge. This means having a sustainable support system in place prior

[39] PR Newswire Europe, "The U.S. Addiction Rehab Industry," *MarketWatch.com*, August 4, 2014, www.marketwatch.com/press-release/the-us-addiction-rehab-industry-2014-08-04-52033057.

[40] National Institute on Drug Abuse, "Treatment and Recovery," *Drug, Brains, and Behavior: The Science of Addiction*, updated July 2018, www.drugabuse.gov/publications/drugs-brains-behavior-science-addiction/treatment-recovery.

to discharge, and a few hours of aftercare and one therapy session a week won't cut it.

Some facilities have inadequate staffing (psychiatrists, licensed experienced psychotherapists) and overstep the limits of their capabilities. Most addiction counselors and treatment centers view addiction as the insanity of doing the same thing again and again and expecting different results, but that is precisely what they are doing when they offer the patient the same failed treatment plan again and again, then expect different results. This presents a huge financial burden on patients and insurance companies, but even worse, it deepens the patient's probability of failure and sense of hopelessness. It's one thing to go to a few meetings and relapse, but it's emotionally devastating to spend a month or more of your life and, in many cases, invest upward of tens of thousands of dollars in treatment at a facility and fail. Also, since A.A., outpatient, and inpatient programs can't accurately track how many people stay sober and how many people relapse, there's not much data to support that residential treatment is any better than outside help. If a patient can't stay sober in outpatient treatment, I'm all for residential, but if residential didn't work the first time, Plan B should be different than Plan A—like long-term detox or daily therapy combined with a sober-living facility if necessary.

One key reason for the immense relapse rate is that treatment centers tend to ignore that addicts usually don't remain pigeonholed in one addictive pattern. To cease one addictive behavior isn't like swatting a mosquito and abolishing all insects once and for all. It's more like the Whac-A-Mole game. You smash down your addiction to alcohol, and next thing you know, you've become addicted to caffeine or cigarettes—a maze is a maze is a maze.

It's not unusual for a person in treatment to smoke like a chimney, drink ten cups of coffee a day, or dive into love or sex addiction while being treated for alcoholism or drug abuse—right at the facility. Treatment generally focuses on one specific behavior and fails to recognize that all addictive behaviors exist for one reason—to seemingly get rid of unwanted feelings or obtain a more positive state of mind. This approach comes from a reluctance to separate the addict from all of their vices at once.

"First things first" is the standard. Best that the addict not feel overwhelmed. But what I've found both in my practice and my personal experience is that no one can get completely well unless they first become unhinged then put back together, and there is no better place to do this than in treatment. Perhaps the real issue is the fear that no one would sign up.

But consider this: Becoming unhinged doesn't mean just falling apart. It means disconnecting from the addictive pattern itself and all of its manifestations. To do this, we must remove all the false comforts of substitute addiction and go right to the source. Healing from within is the only way to true freedom. More on this to come.

I recommend treatment only when it's in the patient's best interest to be removed from an unsafe environment or other methods of abstinence have failed. I carefully recommend a facility that is local so the patient has a support system on departure, and one that will collaborate on and follow through with the patient's aftercare plan.

Behavior Modification

I'm not going to bother reviewing all of the different types of behavior modification programs that have failed (such as "controlled drinking"). Typically, controlled use is measured intake. The patient keeps a chart of agreed upon usage and is positively reinforced (intrinsically or otherwise) by sticking to that agreement.

Another method of controlled drinking is aversion therapy, pairing a negative stimulus with the addiction of choice. For example, patients are shown pictures of a skull and crossbones next to a bottle of alcohol or given a mild electric shock every time they see a drink. Of course, every addict has already experienced enough shock, and it hasn't stopped them from drinking; it's only created a greater need to continue self-medicating.

I've worked with thousands of people who were addicted, and I've never seen anyone control their addiction for very long. The fact that they've lost control is what defines their addicted status. If a gambler could bet five dollars and walk away, she'd have accomplished that on her own. If a porn addict could control himself, he would have stopped before he got fired for using porn at work. Attempting to control any un-controllable behavior is like teaching the mouse to have a little bite of the cheese, leave it, and make its way out of the maze.

The two most commonly used and effective methods for behavior modification are cognitive therapy and 12-Step programs.

Cognitive Therapy: Cognitive therapy helps people change their thoughts and regulate their feelings so they can change the behavior that is triggered by those thoughts and feelings. *Rational-emotive therapy*, developed by Dr. Albert Ellis, and other cognitive therapies are commonly used to treat addiction by teaching patients how to recognize that their unpleasant thoughts produce unpleasant feelings. By reorganizing the irrational beliefs and replacing them with more rational thoughts, feelings would improve and thus remove the need to self-medicate. Cognitive therapy is an effective way to help people become more rational and be better thinkers, but it does not heal the wounds underneath the addiction, so it does not provide a cure. "If a bad feeling activates my addiction, I can rethink my way into a better feeling, and I won't want to act out," says the patient.

While cognitive therapy is a good adjunct tool for abstinence, it is not the end-all treatment. When a person attempts to cover an unhealed wound with cognitive behavioral techniques, it is like putting pink frosting on a mud pie. The unhealed wound festers, and the addictive behavior either resumes in its original form or shapeshifts into a new "drug" of choice, and the person becomes sucked back into the maze. Cognitive therapy is a good first step at stopping an addiction, if followed by the necessary steps to heal the underlying wound.

SMART Recovery is also a cognitive-based treatment to manage thoughts and feelings, but it also addresses motivation, urges to use, and a balanced life. The group meetings are held once or twice weekly, have a trained group facilitator, and are free of charge. A downside of SMART Recovery is that the one or two weekly meetings are not enough for people whose addiction is constantly gnawing at them.

12-Step Programs: The original 12-Step program of Alcoholics Anonymous was founded in 1935 when a few people, having gone through every imaginable attempt at sobriety, became able to maintain abstinence through a behavioral and spiritual program that involved the admission of powerlessness, willingness to be abstinent, righting their wrongs, and finding a connection to a "higher power." A.A. views alcoholism as a mental obsession, physical addiction, and spiritual void. From my observations, the "willingness to ask a higher power to remove the obsession" to partake of the addiction has been extremely successful for those who follow this suggestion.

Since the first A.A. meeting, 12-Step meetings have popped up worldwide for every addiction imaginable. Attended by millions, meetings are ubiquitous—live or online—and cost nothing. In my opinion the 12-Step program, when followed, is more effective for *obtaining* abstinence than any other form of treatment. Recent research has concluded that spiritual- and religious-based interventions are more effective at reducing or eliminating substance use and equally as effective as other programs on broader measures of wellness and function.[41]

A.A. reports a 50 percent success rate, with about 25 percent of the successes occurring after numerous attempts,[42] though many of these folks may continue to go on and off the wagon.

---

[41] American Psychiatric Association Staff, "Twelve-Step-Based Programs Effective for Substance Abuse Problems," *APA Blogs*, September 3, 2019, www.psychiatry.org/news-room/apa-blogs/apa-blog/2019/09/twelve-step-based-programs-effective-for-substance-use-problems.

[42] Nicolle Monico and Scot Thomas, "The 12 Steps of Alcoholics Anonymous (AA)," July 14, 2019, *Alcohol.org*, https://www.alcohol.org/alcoholics-anonymous/.

The 12 Steps are an excellent way to stop a behavior and develop a solid support system, but the program falls short when it comes to addressing the trauma that underlies most addictive behavior. When asked to do a moral inventory and find "your own role" in painful relationships, it is not likely to uncover or address the original wound that led to the whole mess in the first place. The 12-Step programs do recommend "outside help" for people who suffer emotional or mental disorders. In my opinion, that would be almost every addict. Children are not the cause of their own abuse or neglect. Glossing over the pain only drives the memory of trauma deeper into the unconscious mind. Consequently, people either suffer chronic relapses, or they stay sober but become addicted to something else, and/or remain miserable.

Outpatient Psychotherapy

There are many types of professionals who offer outpatient psychotherapy; each one has benefits as well as limitations.

Psychiatrists are medical doctors who specialize in psychiatry and who tend to treat most psychiatric disorders with medication. Unlike the founders of psychotherapy, Sigmund Freud and his followers, most psychiatrists today do not offer psychotherapy. When treating addiction, psychiatrists write prescriptions to help patients reduce the withdrawal effects or substitute one drug for a less addictive one, or they prescribe Antabuse, which causes violent nausea when mixed with alcohol. A psychiatrist also will screen for a psychiatric diagnosis other than the addiction. I carefully select the psychiatrist with whom I work, so that we can collaborate on treatment. I will cover this in greater detail later on.

Psychologists have doctorate degrees in psychology, and counselors have master's degrees in mental health, psychology, or a related field such as social work. None is specifically trained in addictions, nor can they prescribe medication. I have seen numerous patients who were substance abusers and went for years to a psychologist and mental health counselor who knew little to nothing about the symptoms of addiction, so it was never addressed.

Addiction counselors usually have either two-year or four-year degrees in addictions and are either certified or licensed in that field. The complexity of sorting out pathology from addiction is not a simple matter. Addiction counselors are trained to diagnose and counsel people on how to stay sober. They are not trained to diagnose or treat personality disorders: narcissism or borderline, antisocial, or paranoid personalities. Nor are they trained to treat mental illness such as schizophrenia, manic-depression, major depressive disorders, or psychosis, all of which require that the patient be on medication to be able to perform life's daily tasks and functions.

Addiction counselors are not trained to discern the difference between an organic psychosis and a drug-induced psychosis. Research has indicated a link between young pot users and schizophrenic-like symptoms.[43] For example, I have treated several young men who were diagnosed with schizophrenia, but who were in fact addicted to marijuana, and when they stopped

---

[43] Tim Newman, "Cannabis and Schizophrenia: New Evidence Unveiled," *Medical News Today*, April 28, 2017, www.medicalnewstoday.com/articles/317170.php.

using, the schizophrenic symptoms stopped. This misdiagnosis is common, and these types of situations require a
psychiatrist's evaluation to be sure.

As one example, John was brought to therapy by his uncle
because he was "acting strange." John had been talking about
aliens and was writing nonsensical things in his notebook.
He also thought he was a unique species of human who
could breathe underneath the water. All of these are schizophrenic-like symptoms, but John had had no prior episodes
of psychosis.

However, John had used large quantities of both marijuana
and hallucinogens. He reported, and his uncle confirmed, that
he had been in A.A. for six months, and yet he was psychotic.
John's symptoms were inexplicable, and I referred him to the
psychiatrist with whom I consult and who is a highly skilled
diagnostician. He was unsure whether John's psychosis was
organic or the result of drug use, but he prescribed him the
appropriate medication, so John could be stabilized. After six
months, John was weaned off the medication to see if his
symptoms would return. When they did not, we were able to
draw the conclusion that his symptoms were most likely due
to his prior drug use. To be on the safe side, John continued
to meet with the psychiatrist every few months.

Psychoanalysts are either licensed in psychiatry, psychology,
or mental health and are required to complete several years
of postgraduate education, supervision, and personal psychoanalysis. Treatment is targeted at addressing the underlying
causes of emotional disorders, and psychoanalysts must go
through their own personal psychoanalysis before certification—at least three or more sessions per week for usually a

minimum of four years. I'd like to point out that psychoanalysts are the only licensed professionals who are required to have had therapy prior to certification. This means that many counselors could be unhealthier than the people they are treating. I've often worked with people who, prior to seeing me, were in psychoanalysis for years, who drank and used drugs (or were otherwise addicted) on their way through the process with the other analysts. They might have connected the dots of the precipitating factors of their addiction, but they were still actively using and too numb or shut down to grieve, and they remained unhealed and addicted. This goes to show once again how even psychotherapists who have undergone their own analysis do not always see addiction when it is right in front of them.

Confused? Welcome to my world. I haven't even introduced the other types of licensed or certified addiction professionals: nurse practitioners, psychiatric nurses, educational psychologists, certified life coaches, guidance counselors, hypnotherapists, and sponsors, all with varying degrees of education and training in addiction diagnosis and treatment. All are well-meaning and all have their own *opinions that, in many cases, are freely offered to the same patient.* With all the conflicting advice and variations in diagnosis, it is no wonder that people struggling with addiction are in a maze. I ran around in the maze a long time before I was able to put it all together.

CHAPTER FOUR

WHY TREATMENT FAILS

*Failure is not a single, cataclysmic event. … Failure is nothing
more than a few errors in judgment repeated every day.*
—Jim Rohn

According to the National Institute on Drug Abuse, the
relapse rate for people who go to treatment is between
40 percent and 60 percent,[44] not much different than those
who attend 12-Step meetings with a relapse rate of at least 50
percent.[45] It is difficult to track the actual rates of most individuals because A.A. does not keep records, and regardless of the
type of treatment, it's not uncommon for someone to have
difficulty stopping the addictive behavior on the first attempt.
Addiction is synonymous with isolation; there must be a
caring support system in place for long-term sobriety. Without
a fulfilling life and healthy bonding, the addict with go back to
the predictable escape into the maze.

---

[44] National Institute on Drug Abuse, "Treatment and Recovery," *Drug, Brains, and
Behavior: The Science of Addiction,* updated July 2018, www.drugabuse.gov/
publications/drugs-brains-behavior-science-addiction/treatment-recovery.
[45] Dan Wagener, "What Is the Success Rate of AA?" *AmericanAddictionCenters.org,*
updated July 17, 2019, www.americanaddictioncenters.org/rehab-guide/12-
step/whats-the-success-rate-of-aa.

One reason for this is that when people leave treatment, often they return to the same environment with the same enablers and/or active addicts. Patients discharged to unsupportive environments are likely to relapse. This is why I believe it is useless to treat an addict without the whole family having treatment as well. It is a difficult adjustment for an addict to be stone sober or otherwise abstinent from other addictions and return to the same dysfunctional household. It is painful for a patient to get sober then reunite with a partner who thinks things will automatically improve. They won't, and both people need help.

An adolescent returned to the same dysfunctional family where the pain began will suffer and is virtually certain to relapse. Judith brought her son, Randy, to therapy because, after several residential treatments and two years of sobriety, he had relapsed. In the session, Randy reported to me that he'd been sexually abused in his early childhood, and his brother had died of an overdose six months prior.

During that initial interview, it was clear to me that even though Judith had brought her son to therapy, she was emotionally disconnected from the seriousness of her son's condition. Randy repeatedly said he needed help, and he knew he was relapsing because of the sexual abuse. Judith never asked him who had sexually abused him or when. When I asked Randy if he wanted to talk about it, he agreed to come back for another session. I spent the remainder of the first session stressing to both of them the importance of immediate and intensive therapy, especially since the combination of Randy having lost a brother to an overdose and being sexually abused put him at an exceptionally high risk.

However, when I asked to see Randy the next day, neither Randy nor his mother thought it necessary to return so soon. When he missed his appointment the following Monday and did not return my calls, I contacted his mother. She told me he was sleeping. I stressed the urgency of seeing him soon, and Judith said she'd tell him. Neither of them ever called back, and they ignored my calls to them, so I had to let it go.

Since Randy was an adult, I could not get help from Child Protective Services and since he was not overtly suicidal, I could not have him committed. I could only feel appalled and pained that Randy might become another overdose statistic— that his mother might lose another son—and there was nothing she was going to do to stop it.

Families aren't the only threat to recovery. Physicians often are the cause of relapse. One patient, Dean, while being scheduled to have knee replacement surgery, was prescribed ninety doses of OxyContin for postsurgical pain. He explained to his doctor that he was in recovery and could not take narcotics. The surgeon's nurse told him that he had to take the pills and specifically, "You have to stay in front of the pain or you will get addicted." When he tried to explain to her that he was already addicted to all mood-altering substances, she told him, "If you don't take the medication, you won't be able to do the physical therapy and won't heal properly."

That's all Dean needed to hear; after all, the doctor knows best. I could not convince Dean to follow the protocol for recovering addicts, which is to have someone else administer the dose as prescribed, and after a week or two, switch to a nonnarcotic pain reliever. By the time Dean came back to therapy, he'd finished the first ninety pills and had filled a second prescription. Two years later, he was still on the same dosage of one pill every four hours. Thankfully, Dean stayed in therapy and was finally able to get detoxed from the OxyContin and back into recovery. I have seen dozens of cases where physicians have sabotaged a person's recovery, and I find it bordering on criminal negligence.

As previously mentioned, unknowing therapists are also a significant contributor to relapse. Shocking as it is, therapists often make the error of telling a patient in recovery that they are not an addict or alcoholic. Denial is the primary defense mechanism that keeps the addict going. When the professional is also in denial and tells a recovering person that they are not addicted, the relapse wheels are set in motion. Even my own psychoanalyst, with whom I spent thirteen years, repeatedly told me she did not think I was an alcoholic, even though I told her I'd been in recovery for many years prior to my analysis. She could not see beyond her own level of understanding. Like so many other therapists, her mental image of someone addicted to substances was more like a person you'd see on the TV show *Intervention*—someone using around the clock or who has hit rock bottom. In reality, according to the National Institutes of Health, 20 percent of all alcoholics are highly functioning.[46] If you add up all the addicts hooked on other types of legal drugs, you'll get a number a lot higher than that. If we remember that addiction (like any illness) is progressive, and someone doesn't have to be homeless before they've contracted the disease, then we will do a better job at

[46] National Institutes of Health, "Researchers Identify Alcoholism Subtypes," *NIH.gov*, June 28, 2007, www.nih.gov/news-events/news-releases/researchers-identify-alcoholism-subtypes.

seeing it and treating it early on. No therapist should ever tell recovering patients they are not addicted.

When dual-diagnosed patients go off their psychotropic medication, they are likely to relapse. Believe it or not, many therapists tell patients they don't need to be on medication for psychosis. When someone sinks into a major depressive-suicidal episode, goes on a manic spending spree, thinks they can fly off of a building or communicate with extraterrestrials, or becomes otherwise psychotic, the therapist will quickly discover why the patient needs medication. Unfortunately, by then it is often too late; the patient has resumed the addiction in an attempt to modulate their symptoms. A patient should never go off meds unless under the supervision of a (addiction-trained) psychiatrist.

Enablers are often the key catalysts of relapse. It is typical for a loved one to either consciously or unconsciously sabotage a patient's recovery. I once treated a family where the mother constantly undermined her young son's recovery. In spite of all of the education and evidence presented to her by his behavior—drug dealing, binge drinking, a near-death experience, marijuana psychosis—she insisted on telling her son he did not have a problem. She refused to go to Al-Anon (the 12-Step program for loved ones of the addicted) or read any of the educational materials I provided. She even went so far as to encourage her son to have a "little drink" on his first A.A. anniversary and on his second one as well. Obliging his pusillanimous mother, who was too frightened to face either the threat of her own possible dependency on alcohol or the threat of losing control over her son, he relapsed both times under her urging. Sadly, it is far too common that parents are unwilling to go for the help they need to best help their children, and they often fail to realize this mistake until it is too late.

In other families, food addicts are tempted with their favorite dishes, sex addicts are tempted with triggers such as a partner suggesting they watch porn, gamblers and work addicts are tempted by a family member who complains about financial lack. Enablers unconsciously sabotage the recovering person because the addict's recovery threatens the enablers' codependency. Someone who has been taking care of the addict may feel less needed, fear abandonment, or even feel resentful and threatened by the change—the loss of control. Sometimes they will go so far as to tell the newly sober person, "I liked you better when you were high," and the recovering addict is too miserable, raw, and vulnerable to remain resolute.

Wounded Healers

Wounded patients who don't receive proper care aren't the only problem. Another reason so many mental health professionals have been unable to treat addicted patients successfully is the failure to see their own addictions and unhealed wounds. I've personally known more therapists who were heavy drug and alcohol users than not. Many people are interested in the field of psychology because of their own childhood trauma, and they have empathy for other people who have suffered similar experiences. It's not enough to care about someone else. If you haven't taken the time or done the work to heal yourself, your ability to help anyone else is limited. The tendency to overlook traits in oneself that you can clearly see in others is far too common in the addiction treatment community. I've counseled many clinicians who thought they were "recovered" only to reveal they were beholden to various addictions including addictive relationships, caffeine, gambling, pornography, sugar, Tinder hookups, video gaming, work, or anything else that would provide a source of superficial relief from their own emotional wounds.

Licensed psychiatrists and therapists must pass all sorts of tests to receive their qualifications, yet they are never required to have their own mental health evaluated or examined for possible addictions. Yet they are allowed to go out into their communities and work with the public. Our communities need therapists who have done the work, healed their wounds, and are empowered role models, not co-addicts steeped in their own denial. If a patient is stuck in a maze looking for a lever, it's not very likely that the therapist will be able to help them see the exit when they both are stuck in the same maze. Patients cannot get well if the people helping them are not well. I often say kids can only be as healthy as their healthiest role model. The same is true of patients.

Sober vs. Well

A person can stop an addiction and be sober without getting well. A person can be sober for many years and still be as emotionally unhealthy as the first day of sobriety. Being well means that you have healed the underlying cause of the addiction and thus have removed the need to use anything or anyone to pacify relentless internal pain. Until addiction is treated as a symptom of the emotional damage it represents, it is unlikely the relapse rate will decline. Until we address the cause, the best we can hope for is to leave the recovering person to remain discontent and unlikely to form the intimate bonds that are natural to those who are not only sober but who are also recovered from their emotional wounds.

Of all the reasons for relapse, the primary cause is underlying the addiction itself—the originating wound remains unhealed. When a child suffers trauma that remains unhealed, it becomes a wound like a huge emotional bruise that needs constant soothing. Until that original wound is healed, the addiction will substitute temporary soothing for actual healing.

Recap

To sum it all up, here's where we currently stand in the field of addictions. The experts lack a consensus on naming the illness and lack agreement on symptoms; thus, addictions often go undiagnosed. Failure to diagnose is arguably the greatest barrier to effective treatment. If you don't know you have it, it can't be treated.

When a proper diagnosis is made, the prescribed treatments include a broad range of options including self-talk, 12-Step meetings, outpatient therapy, and long-term residential treatment, yet every one of these has a high rate of relapse. This is partly due to the fact that the people assigned to treat addiction are not properly trained to do so. Treatment success also is hindered when therapists are sicker than the patients and have yet to address or heal their own emotional wounds. Another common block to successful treatment is that patients are not properly screened for dual diagnosis (i.e., identifying a mental illness or other addictive behaviors). As a result, conditions such as schizophrenia and manic-depression, which require medication, go untreated. This blocks even the best trained mental health professional from being able to support the person in addiction recovery. Further, looking at only part of the picture makes it likely that the patient will fall into a complementary addictive behavior while they are in treatment for the primary one (for example, taking up caffeine, eating, smoking, or sex addiction while addressing alcohol or drug addiction). When patients aren't afforded the opportunity to address all their addictive behaviors simultaneously, this, too, gravely inhibits any chance of long-term recovery.

Another common reason for the high failure rate is that patients are repeatedly sent back into the same environment in which they used. Some treatment centers are more concerned with the bottom-line profit than what's best for the patient. Unless the entire family system is helped, the patient is likely to relapse. We need to change the way we are treating addiction. Under the current model, we aren't leading people out of the maze. We are merely adding more corridors.

Finally, the biggest reason that treatment fails is because the underlying wound is never healed—and unless the patient wants to heal, the treatment will always fail.

A Change in Perspective

It is not my intention or desire to attack the people who are treating addiction, or the models they use. We cannot blame the people who have tried to help. Nor should we blame the doctors, advertisers, drug dealers, or sales reps who sell our society on the idea that the solution to our unhappiness, empty feeling, or whatever discomfort we experience can be found in a pill, a toke, a shot, a sports car, or any other distraction.

All in all, we've settled for something that makes us feel better in the moment rather than something that actually makes us better. We've settled for "getting relief" rather than being well. We've settled for "getting sober" over being happy and fulfilled.

Treating addiction can't be about doing the same thing while we watch people get sicker and even die. It can't be just about making money. We're talking about the tens of thousands of young kids who are dropping dead, daily. We're talking about people who lose everything because they've gambled it away, spent it all on sex, or eaten themselves to death. We're talking about families who are broken, not because of incompatibility but due to an addiction. We're talking about people who never achieve their purpose here because their bodies and minds have been hijacked. We're talking about the fact that addiction is the world's biggest killer. If you get right down to it, almost all premature deaths are due to some type of addiction.

The time has come to take down the wall of pathological resistance and see the truth—that we have become a highly addicted society. We need to face the reality that we are addicted and that we remain addicted because we don't want to deal with our feelings. If we are ever to break free of addiction and reclaim our lives, we must each, as individuals, be willing to accept that the only way we can exit the maze is to address the real cause.

It's time to end the insanity. It's time we provide a clear definition of addiction and provide a treatment plan that works.

The same authorities who provide the diagnosis criteria for addiction, but don't call it that, are the same authorities who say you can never be cured. Even if "once an addict, always an addict" is true, why should we stop there?

If you are struggling with addiction or suspect you might be, I want to show you there is a solution that goes beyond mere abstinence—that transcends the current diagnosis and treatment models. I'm inviting you to go beyond the need to reach outside yourself for something to make you feel better. I invite you to travel the path inward to a place where you can experience a sense of peace and contentment anytime you choose, a place that can never be attained through the pacifying substitutes you have accepted all of your life.

This path can lead way beyond the idea of the "quick fix." It goes deeper than the strategy of using willpower to overcome cravings or to temper a constant state of need. But before you can give yourself that experience, we have to go into that place that has pulled you into feeling you need the quick fix, then find that place inside of you that *can* be "cured."

It's time to get out of the maze for good. The easiest way to find a way out of the maze is to take a bird's-eye view where you can see the whole picture. From that vantage, you can see where the exit is, and you can see a path to get there.

Here are a few questions to give you a better sense of where you might have been stuck and the things that haven't worked up to this point.

Self-Evaluation Questionnaire

1. Have you been trying to get help for a long time?

2. Do you feel like you've tried many different ways to feel better, but for some reason you're stuck?

3. Have you had therapy or are you in recovery but still feel like something's missing? Describe what you mean.

4. Have you lost faith in the therapy? If so, why?

5. Do you feel hopeless to ever get better? If so, what would need to change for you to regain hope?

6. Did you read anything in Part I that specifically applies to you? If so, make a note of it.

PART II

ONE CAUSE

Picture if you will that you are a scientist standing over a maze with a mouse running through it. As you look down, right in the middle of the maze, you see a black hole. Around that black hole is a vortex. As you look into the vortex, you see a circle of dark energy surrounded by a mass of clouds and electrical storms swirling around the hole. Everything that goes near the hole is sucked into the vortex, making it part of an ever-growing darkness. Light cannot enter or escape. The mouse is so busy searching for its "reward," it doesn't notice the hole is growing. Nor is the mouse aware that, left unchecked, the entire maze and everything in it, can be sucked into the hole.

Deep into the center of the black hole is where the cause of addiction resides. In these next chapters, we will enter the hole together, so you can see what's there and find a way out.

CHAPTER FIVE

WHERE ADDICTION STARTS

*Although it pains me to admit it, I am quite familiar with the
holes in life. And this familiarity is due to the fact that I spend
far more time in these holes than I spend on the paths that
brought me to them.*
—Craig D. Lounsbrough

We're all born with a natural tendency toward happiness—
to feel good in our own skin. Every newborn is
hardwired for happiness and success. It is the natural state of
being human. Yet the fact of life is that trauma happens.
Disappointment happens. Pain, sorrow, and loss happen. But
no matter how brutal, awful, or intense the pain suffered,
trauma itself does not cause addiction. Trauma unaddressed
does. Unhealed emotional trauma becomes the wound that
creates a persistent ache, pain, or craving that calls for relief.
This is why so many of us turn to substances or activities that
numb, because we want to blot out that residual pain.

The residual pain of trauma (physical or emotional) is
there because it was never dealt with on the emotional level.
It got buried alive, so trauma seeps into our consciousness as

a constant ache or an unshakable feeling of emptiness, a void that, despite repeated and misguided efforts, cannot be filled. Or at least it can seem that way.

When my patients first attempt to stop an addiction, they report the same feelings: "I feel hollow inside," "I feel like the wind blows through me," "I feel like an empty statue." Underlying all addictions is a battle—a person is fighting intolerable feelings and attempting to fill a gnawing, persistent, invisible hole.

What few ever come to realize is that the pain or emptiness persists because it is acting as an alarm, attempting to tell us that our emotional heart has been bruised and needs attention. The empty feeling is asking us to turn inward and give ourselves more love. But instead, we douse ourselves with drugs and anything else that will distract, but only reinjure, us. These actions merely compound the trauma and intensify the feeling of emptiness. This is also why the deeper one goes into addiction, the greater the pain, the greater the emptiness. It's telling us that we're going in the wrong direction. I call it the invisible hole, because we can feel it all the time, but while we are caught in the maze of addiction, we can't see it.

A Hole to Fill

If you're addicted or suspect you are, know that long before you developed even an inkling that something like addiction could happen to you, you probably noticed a feeling of being disconnected from yourself and/or others—as if you were someone different or defective. When you were young, you might have felt you were born into the wrong family, since everyone seemed to fit in but you. You might have suffered abuse. Perhaps members of your family were unhappy, and you felt responsible for making everyone feel better, only to feel sad when things did not improve. Maybe you were shy and spent hours alone wondering why everyone had friends but you. Perhaps you had all the material things in life, but you were discontent. You might have craved affection and intimacy from distant, unaffectionate parents, causing you to seek that missing touch with people who hurt you or took advantage. Perhaps you lost a parent and felt depressed and alone, with no one to share your grief.

Whatever the original trauma, realize that over time, that initial sense of unease grew and became what I call "the invisible hole," a persistent, unrelenting sense of pain and emptiness that I believe is the driving force behind all manifestations of addiction. Regardless of the particular form or expression, if you look closely, you will see that addiction originates here. It is the invisible hole that causes you to search for ways to escape the pain left by some unmet need or betrayal during your childhood.

Children are born completely helpless and dependent upon their caregivers for survival. Children are wired to seek a connection with and the approval of their parents. Because babies are totally dependent, any perceived lack of approval or insufficient nurturing can be viewed as a direct threat to their survival. No parenting is perfect, but if children are shown again and again that being loved is conditional and that they are not OK as they are, an invisible hole forms, and the child's psyche becomes vulnerable to addiction.

It is my belief that a child who has a genetic predisposition to addiction is not doomed to develop those traits unless they also experience trauma that goes untreated and unhealed. Many recovering alcoholics have educated their children about addiction, making them aware of the possibility that they may have a predisposition to developing an addiction. But in the absence of an unhealed trauma, no invisible hole will be formed, and without the invisible hole, addictive behaviors don't hold the same allure. If people feel whole and complete within themselves and notice that their actions look like addictive behavior, they'll stop. They will recognize it's not good for them, and they will walk away unscathed.

Unfortunately, the all-too-common combination of ineffective parenting strategies and growing up in an addicted society predisposes children to grow into addicted adults. Children who grow up with addicted parents are more likely to emulate the behavior they observe. Often parents unwittingly model or encourage behavior that sets in motion ineffective coping strategies. A mother who consoles her troubled child with food teaches her child that food will make the hurt go away, and the child will grow up and seek food for comfort, rather than offer soothing words and hugs to themselves or receive the comfort of others.

Social programming also is a huge factor in setting up kids for addiction. From the time children start watching television, they see images of ways to "feel good": the extra-cheesy pizza is extra-cheesy festive; the little pill removes all worries and turns your frowny face into a smiley one; the sexy new car and the icy bottle of beer make you more desirable to hot men or women. All of these messages convey to impressionable minds that they need to get something from the outside to feel OK on the inside. Few advertisements convey the idea that these are things to enjoy and are not here to complete us. No one sets out to become an addict; it catches us off guard. An addiction can happen quickly or slowly and can affect anyone regardless of intelligence, social class, ethnic group, or religion. One cigarette a day becomes four then becomes a pack or more. One drink a day becomes a few then becomes a quart or more. A few extra pounds become ten then fifty or more. If this reminds you of your experience, consider you might also have thought you were in control at first, but all the while, you were already trapped. By the time you realized you had a problem, you were already in the maze.

"Next time will be different" was your motto as you swore off alcohol, porn, spending, or whatever else lured you in. Time and time again, no amount of guilt ever reformed you; it only took you further down. You convinced yourself your "bad habits" had nothing to do with lost loves, careers, or people who betrayed you. As everything you valued in life slipped through your fingers, you still might have thought you had control. If any of this sounds familiar, embrace the aware-ness. There's no need to feel ashamed. This is a common scenario, and it can happen to anyone.

I have a dear friend, a Harvard graduate who lost his medical practice and his wife to alcohol. Later, after getting sober, he started a new life at a state university doing research, but he began to drink again. He has been featured twice in his town newspaper: once for driving his car into a storefront and once for threatening to shoot his former friend. But he still thought he was in control, even as his addiction was consuming him once again. As I write this, he still has not sought help. I hope he does, but I fear that he, like so many others, has been swallowed by the disease.

Some manifestations of addiction are more socially acceptable than others; some are uglier, messier, or more violent, but they all serve the same purpose. A person who chews gum incessantly might not be viewed socially in the same way as the person who suffers from debilitating drug dependence. But in all cases, addicts who are not satisfying their urges will suffer emotional stress—anger, agitation, moodiness—until their cravings are met. We all recognize that taking away someone's cigarettes or booze will make them anxious, upset, and moody. But try taking chewing gum from someone who uses it for oral gratification or asking a compulsively neat person to leave the house messy for a whole day and see what happens. You will observe the same anxiety, anger, and discontent. Regardless of which pacifier they use, addicts will experience similar emotional withdrawal symptoms in one form or another, because each is using their "drug of choice" in an attempt to fill the same invisible hole.

The guy driving his Rolls-Royce might not see he's in the same addiction hole when he pulls up next to someone strung out on drugs holding a sign that reads, "Will Work for Food." But if the luxury car owner has just come off an eighty-hour workweek and is on his way to the nearest strip club for a night of boozing and lap dances, he might indeed be embroiled in exactly the same struggle. Same disease, different costumes.

Regardless of the form it takes, there is only one addiction, and it is coming from the same urge to fill that imaginary hole—the one formed in that moment in time when a person suffered a hurt that left them with a feeling of being less than, of being unlovable, of not being enough, or of feeling worthless, then tried to cover up or fill the hole left by that pain with something that would make it go away. But that hole cannot be filled with drugs or booze or sex or work. And addiction can't be solved by mere abstinence either.

Why Abstinence Fails

Abstinence is an excellent place to start the healing process, but the person who is attempting to recover from addiction through abstinence likely will find they've underestimated its versatility. For example, if you were ever a smoker, you might think that by giving up cigarettes, you gave up your addiction. But think again. Did you take up chewing gum? Sucking on Jolly Ranchers? Eating? What new behavior did you pick up to offset or distract you from your cravings?

Addiction is a signal from your unconscious there is a deep hurt inside you that needs to be healed. The goal, from a subconscious point of view, is to get you to heal. And it is not going to give up trying to get your attention just because you gave up your first-choice distraction. Until the wound is healed, addiction will continue to morph itself and resurface in another form, like the trick a magician plays of hiding an object under one of three cups, and you can never guess which one. Addiction is the object that appears to have magically shifted around. The object is always there, but you never know where it will pop up next.

Regardless of the form, driven by the same unresolved pain, all forms of addiction offer the illusion that the empty feeling has disappeared—temporarily, at least. We get lured in, looking for the right fix—a few drinks, a joint, a container of ice cream, a new relationship. When we relate to people, places, and things as ways to fill an invisible hole, we remain in the maze.

Rather than focus on the specific behavior, the best way to know if you're addicted is to do a gut check to see how you feel when you are not using. You might feel as if you are floating in a place of nothingness or that you don't even know yourself anymore. You might feel that you are invisible, and no one sees you. You might feel dead inside, and the diminishing life spark inside you can be ignited only with the next drink or drug dose. You might feel that your addiction is the only thing you can look forward to in your desolate, solitary life. You might have spent years in recovery meetings, and yet wonder why you are not "happy, joyous, and free." You might be haunted by a persistent feeling of inauthenticity.

The Way Out

When we're addicted, it is as though we walk around holding a cord looking for the next place to plug in and fill up. Hypnotized into believing that somehow "garbage in" will fill the invisible hole, we keep searching the garbage can for the next quick fix—rather than trying to understand how the hole got there in the first place. Hypnotized into believing that toxins, poisons, and super thrills are fun and good for us, we are oblivious to all the warning signs. We are addicted before we ever realize that the only thing we accomplish by "indulging" in all these distractions is expanding the vortex of pain. And the only reason that discomfort exists is to point out that we have a wound, and we need to heal it.

Even if you are in recovery and you are still unhappy, I want you to know that there is hope. There is one way out.

There is *only* one way out of the maze of addiction, and it's not to be found on the other side at the perimeter. The illusion that you can exit the maze at the same place you entered will not lead to a way out, but will merely cause you to reenact the trauma that put you there.

The invisible hole that represents the swirling storm that was formed over a lifetime of painful experiences must be faced. If you want to heal, you must go into the center and enter the vortex where the root of all your pain and trauma resides.

Like Luke Skywalker in *Star Wars* had to go into the swamp and face the demons of his past before Yoda could help him gather his power, you, too, must go into the painful past and penetrate the wound before you can fully heal and find your true power. I'm not going to lie. It is an uncomfortable process, but by choosing to love yourself over and over, you can overcome the fear of facing your demons. The following chapters will explain how you can lead yourself out of that nightmare and into a place of fearless love for yourself and others.

Self-Evaluation Questionnaire

1. Do you remember the first time you felt an uneasiness inside you that you wanted to rid yourself of? Describe that experience.

2. When was the first time you turned to something you knew was "bad" (alcohol, cigarettes, sugar, etc.) for "comfort"? What were the circumstances? What did you take? How did it make you feel?

3. What happened after you experienced that first sense of relief from using?

4. Did you soon look forward to the next time? Did the uneasiness and feeling of discontent return? If so, describe what it felt like.

5. Did you notice that the more you tried to fill the empty feeling of the hole, the bigger it grew? If so, describe what happened.

6. List all of the ways you tried to fill the hole.

7. Has the hole gone away? How do you know? If it's still there, how does it feel?

8. Name all of the actions or substances you have used to avoid facing emotional pain.

9. Describe how you felt after you used and the high wore off.

10. Describe what it would feel like to be free of a behavior you'd like to stop.

11. Once the wounds in the invisible hole are healed, what do you want to have in that space?

12. How would it feel to have that void inside of you filled with joy, peace, and contentment?

CHAPTER SIX

HOW THE HOLE BEGAN

There are wounds that never show on the body that are deeper
and more hurtful than anything that bleeds.
—Laurell K. Hamilton

Before we observe how the hole forms in the psyche, we'll need to gain a clear picture of the conditions that create solid self-esteem in a child—the type of personality that has no predisposition to addiction.

First, let's take another look at rats. Since rats are social in nature and have brains that function similarly to a human's, they are often used in experiments to understand human behavior. Both are social, warm-blooded mammals that respond similarly to situations. In a famous study called the "Rat Park" experiment, Bruce Alexander and his colleagues performed an experiment to determine if rats would find highly addictive drugs "irresistible."[47]

---

[47] Bruce Alexander, "Rat Park," *Addiction: The View from Rat Park*, 2010, www.brucekalexander.com/articles-speeches/rat-park/148-addiction-the-view-from-rat-park.

The scientists discovered that rats who were raised in a large box (communal park) with plenty of food, activities, and other rats to play with showed little to no interest in consuming (highly addictive) morphine. These findings were compared with a prior experiment in which rats were kept in solitary confinement in small metal cages. When these rats were offered morphine, they consumed high doses. These results debunked the hypothesis that highly addictive drugs are the problem, because the rats in the park who had all their needs met, including social ones, showed little to no interest in saturating their brains with a mood-altering substance. The results demonstrated that loneliness and lack are the drivers of drug abuse, not the drug itself. Similarly, a child who feels fulfilled will not be susceptible to substitutes for fulfilling experiences—there's no hole to fill.

Ideally, before a baby is conceived, two people who are in love and ready to have a child start to prepare for a new life before the pregnancy ever occurs. They are emotionally and financially stable and feel confident that they are ready to take on the responsibility of childcare (in some cases, it might be a single parent with help) that will span at least two decades. Of course, families have various levels of income, and not all children grow up with financial security. Money is not a requirement to raise a child who feels confident, loved, and lovable.

Before pregnancy, the mother makes sure she is healthy and fit, so her body can properly house and nourish a developing fetus. During pregnancy, the mother's priority is taking care of the fetus: getting enough rest, eating healthy food, and experiencing minimal stress. She does not drink, smoke, or otherwise put toxins in her body. The childbirth is as natural as possible without putting mother or child at risk, with both parents present. The baby is promptly handed over to the mother, who cradles her child and looks into the baby's eyes, while an outpouring of love flows down from both parents. They tell the baby, "We love you; we are so happy you are here."

Again, ideally, the mother breastfeeds so her baby gets the antibodies, colostrum, prebiotics, and other health benefits that are not available in formula.

The baby is brought home to a secure environment, and the mother continues to bond with her child. Her attention is focused on the baby, and she adapts her life to the infant's needs. The child basks in the warmth of the mother's body during feedings, and her primary focus is attuning herself to her baby. The father also bonds with the child by participating as much as possible in the child's care. This baby feels safe, warm, full, and secure. Ideally, extended family members— grandparents, aunts, and uncles, who also provide additional support to the parents—are healthy, balanced individuals adding greater security to the family bond. As the infant grows, the parents continue to adjust to the child's needs, yet they make sure they remain intimate and connected as a couple. Their world rotates around proper care of their offspring, including an environment that stimulates the child's natural curiosity. Advances such as first steps are met with approval and delight. When the infant starts to assert independence, the parents are supportive, teaching the child to be confident that it's safe to break away as a separate person while continuing to receive support.

As the child grows, the parents teach healthy habits of self-care, such as good nutrition, obtaining appropriate mental stimulation, and exercise. Natural talents are cultivated and encouraged. The parents take the time to explain why these things are important to the body and mind, so the child internalizes self-care as an expression of self-respect and self-love. Parents model emotional health when they validate each other and teach the child how to communicate painful feelings naturally—crying when sad and talking out anger rather than acting it out. The parents consistently model healthy behavior in their actions. When the child is ready, sexuality is explained in an age-appropriate context.

These parents do not attempt to rescue their children every time a mistake is made. They allow the child to feel bad about wrong choices, and they allow the child to figure out a way to correct their mistakes. When parents allow their children to experience the consequences of their choices, they are facilitating maturity and independence. Through trial and error, the youth develops the habit of making good decisions without parental interception or intrusion.

As a teenager, a solid inner core has formed, and the youth is able to manage normal social anxiety without the need to go along with the crowd just to feel accepted. The parents explain that all kids feel nervous, and there's no need to drink or use drugs just to feel better or to try and fit in. They explain that it's OK to be a nonjudgmental observer without participating. The child is also encouraged to hang out with other kids who don't drink or use drugs. These kids are nervous, too, but they can manage their social anxiety in a natural way, and they can enjoy time together without getting high.

As a strong sense of self and identity develops, the adolescent begins to form an idea of a future life and career. The child's desires are explored and honored, while the parents provide guidance without imposing their own secret wishes and desires on the child.

This individual grows into a secure adult who feels the world and the people in it are safe. This individual can take life's disappointments, mourn them, learn and grow from them, and move on. Goals are not aborted because of temporary failure, but those setbacks are used to learn and to be better. The young adult learns to navigate their way through life and make the best of it.

While this description might seem otherworldly to many, psychoanalysts starting with Freud have known the importance of a well-developed ego and adjustment to life. There have been countless studies that have validated the importance of healthy childhood development. It does not mean, however, that a healthy childhood is a prerequisite for a fulfilling life, only that you might need to work harder at it if you lacked a solid foundation.

You might be thinking that I'm living in some kind of la-la land and not seeing family life through a realistic lens. After all, with so many different cultures and socioeconomic classes, how can I possibly oversimplify such a complex issue? So, let's be clear: I'm not saying that any childhood has to be (or even should be) perfect, as confronting difficulties is also an important part of becoming a strong and capable adult. But a childhood that is safe enough and fulfilling enough to allow the child to enjoy life without having to engage in artificial "OK-ness" creates a strong foundation for developing a fulfilling life in adulthood. Bottom line: A child has to be provided enough emotional security and empathic involvement either by a parent or a respected role model to grow up with the awareness that they are whole and unbroken. The child who feels cared for and loved will be governed by love rather than pain. Children who grow up in an abusive or neglectful environment most likely will struggle with some manifestation of addiction at some point in their lives—either by being addicted, being attracted to someone who has an addiction, or both.

After reading the above, you can identify some of the things that were missing in your childhood and learn how to better care for yourself now. Many people don't have a clue what it means to love. For starters, you can reread this section and pinpoint specific acts of love that were missing in your childhood. Then you can start to correct those inadequacies with acts of self-love. You are now the adult who meets your own needs in healthy ways, which include allowing others to help you when necessary.

Good Enough, Not Perfect

There is no perfect way to raise a child, and when parents are expecting a new birth, they are not given a how-to manual for raising children. In spite of many imperfections in how a child is raised, children turn out fine. Minor errors are overlooked, and if the big errors are acknowledged and healed, they, too, are left in the past. However, if traumatic moments are not acknowledged and addressed, they fester into a wound that forms the invisible hole that drives addiction.

Let's start off by saying that most caretakers do not intend to harm. Parenting strategies tend to be handed down from one generation to the next. These inherited values and behaviors can set in place all sorts of dysfunctional patterns and beliefs. Worse, children raised in families that were suffering from addiction, mental health problems, and other dysfunctions have the compounded challenge of being at the mercy of people who were too ill to know what they were doing. Children brought up in these environments often find themselves as adults following in the footsteps of the very people they vowed never to emulate. If you are willing to examine what has happened in your family tree, you can be the one to stop the dysfunction for future generations.

Early Trauma and Later Addiction

We now know that abuse can start before a child is even born. A mother who is abusing drugs or alcohol while pregnant, or not taking care of herself in other ways, is exposing her unborn child to the potential risk of permanent damage. For example, a pregnant woman who abuses substances could give birth to a child who suffers from fetal alcohol syndrome or drug dependence, conditions that could affect the baby's neurological and physical well-being for life. If she isn't eating properly or if she's smoking, the developing fetus will be more susceptible to low birth weight, which can increase the risk of psychiatric problems later in life.[48]

If parents are in a combative state during the pregnancy, this causes the release of stress hormones such as adrenaline and cortisol in the mother's body. Excessive amounts of these hormones could result in the child developing mood disorders later.[49]

From the moment of birth, we begin to form our concept of ourselves and our place in the world. When nurtured and taught love and respect for themselves and others, most children will grow up to become well-adjusted and happy adults. When children learn to share and receive love, they will naturally balance the needs of self and others.

Child-rearing errors produce a different result. If a child is abused, neglected, or raised in a home that does not feel safe, that child develops an image of an unsafe world. These children perceive relationships as painful and lacking love, or they grow to believe that life is cruel and a place of lack. Placed in a survival mode, these children grow up feeling a void inside, an inivisible hole that they can't seem to fill no matter what. They are left with an insatiable need, and they usually have no idea why or what the source is. Many people go their entire lives feeling the invisible hole and trying to fill it with addictive behaviors without understanding that their

[48] Karen Matthewson, "Low Birth Weight Babies at Higher Risk for Mental Health Problems Later in Life," American Psychological Association, February 13, 2017, www.apa.org/news/press/releases/2017/02/low-birth-weight.

[49] British Neuroscience Association. "Fetal Exposure to Excessive Stress Hormones in the Womb Linked to Adult Mood Disorders," ScienceDaily, April 7, 2013, www.sciencedaily.com/releases/2013/04/130407090835.htm.

addictive behavior is trying to replace the love and nurturing that was lacking in their childhood.

There is a difference between abuse and trauma. All abuse is traumatic, but not all trauma is abuse. Trauma can be the result of a death of a loved one, an illness that causes a child to miss school and friends, loss of a favorite pet or love object, or any other type of painful event. If a child suffers loss, it is traumatic but not abusive, unless the child is not allowed the opportunity to grieve.

Sometimes a parent will tell a child it's not OK to feel sad when a loss has occurred, or in some other way encourage the child to hide or suppress feelings. The only appropriate reaction to a child's pain is to show empathy, provide comfort, and create an opening for the child to talk about the experience, so the pain is released and moved beyond. If that pain remains unresolved, it turns into suffering and unresolved grief.

An addictive personality develops from unhealed trauma that lodged in the psyche as a wound, which becomes the invisible hole that drives the addiction.

I will not cover every form of abuse that children endure, but if you experienced a deep pain or frightening experience when you were a child, and that wound has not been addressed and healed, consider yourself someone who has carried trauma for your whole life.

I'd like to stress that it is not my intention to blame anyone—that is a rabbit hole with no end. We tend to parent in the same way we were parented. In order to heal, we do have to understand what happened, and until we face that truth, we cannot face the feelings that keep the vortex swirling.

Children are subjected to different types of abuse: emotional, physical, sexual, and verbal as well as neglect. Each of these can occur in varying degrees of intensity and duration, and each can be blatant or subtle. They all fuel the vortex that deepens the sense of emptiness and craving that I call the invisible hole, which lures people into the addiction maze.

Emotional abuse occurs when a child's mind is exposed to cruelty in the form of unfair or inappropriate encounters. For example, a child is deeply saddened and/or scared when witnessing their caretakers engage in violent or excessively loud arguments. Children often come out of these situations feeling that they are responsible for the conflict, separation, or divorce. Another form of emotional abuse is when children are expected to perform tasks and responsibilities beyond their maturity level. No one should expect five-year-olds to cook their own meals or be responsible for major housekeeping, yet this is a frequent occurrence in some households. Parents are supposed to be there for their children, not the other way around.

Emotional blackmail happens when a parent tells a child to help them keep a secret or hide a wrongful act. Children aren't impressed when a parent flaunts an affair, but they do become torn as a witness to this type of betrayal.

Children are emotionally abused when told that their birth was the result of an unplanned pregnancy and a hardship on the family, instilling a feeling of being unwanted burdens. Children who are favored over their siblings by one or both parents feel guilty, and those who are seen as lesser than their sibling(s) feel angry. Either way, blatant favoritism is emotionally abusive.

It is emotionally abusive for a parent to make promises without keeping them, then make the child feel guilty for feeling disappointed. Without providing an adequate reason or simply blowing off any explanation, the parent teaches the child that it's unsafe to trust, and it's wrong to feel disappointed. In either case, raising a child's expectations without delivering and not owning up to the failure to follow through are abusive.

I've heard this typical scenario countless times: A young child waits for a drunk parent to come home, and upon return, the overly cheerful (guilt-ridden) parent apologizes for missing dinner but promises to take the child to buy a new bicycle (or other toy) the following morning. When the parent still hasn't arisen by noon, the frustrated child attempts to awaken the parent, only to be yelled at for the disturbance. As two o'clock rolls around and the parent emerges, the child regains excitement about the new bicycle, but instead of going to the store, they are forced to accompany the parent to the liquor store. When the disappointed child cries and asks about the bicycle, the parent yells at the child for being selfish. This youngster learns not only to distrust but also learns to expect depression and disappointment from a person who is supposed to be trustworthy and whom they had counted on.

Denying what a child accurately sees, hears, or senses, and lying to a child so as to invalidate a child's perception of reality are abuse. When children are micromanaged and trained to act like robots, or overloaded with rules and regulations, their sense of freedom, independence, and spontaneity is squelched. When a child witnesses a parent who becomes intoxicated, steals, or otherwise breaks the law, the child is witnessing a parent who is out of control, thus creating fear and a sense of instability.

Emotional abuse may happen outside of the core family, with other relatives, or within schools or religious institutions. Anyone whose behavior causes a child to feel less than, shameful, or afraid is facilitating abuse rather than inspiration. An angry scowl or dismissive attitude can lower a child's self-concept as much as harsh words. When children are told they are stupid, failures, sinful, or otherwise unacceptable, these messages will penetrate the child's ego and fester as a persistent sense of unworthiness. Withholding love, retaliating, and humiliating children in public are other ways children are made to feel worthless.

Neglect occurs when a child's basic needs for food, shelter, physical safety, and love are not properly met. When funds are available, no child should go hungry or without the nourishment that supports strong physical growth and development. A child should be adequately clothed, sheltered, and raised in a safe and sanitary environment, so that home provides a feeling of physical comfort and safety. Anything less than this is a form of neglect.

Even parents who live in poverty manage to raise children whose basic needs are met. Sometimes they wear clothing that has been donated or eat low-cost foods, but if they still are shown love and concern, these children can grow up to thrive. I have worked with people who knew they had less than their schoolmates, but who felt they received adequate care because a parent made their clothes, cooked delicious but inexpensive meals, and knew how to make a dollar last. I recently read a book about Jackie Robinson and how his mother managed to provide five children with their basic needs without the assistance of welfare.[50] The devotion this mother had for meeting the needs of her children produced a son who is recognized as one of the greatest and most respected men of all time. Parents who are good providers and have the means to offer plenty of material things to their children often neglect to spend adequate time with them. Children raised in families who have an abundance of everything but time, often feel lonely and unloved. When adults don't have time to talk with their children, do things with them, and be there to support them emotionally, the children will feel less important than their parents' preoccupation and priorities. The point I am making here is that when it comes to raising emotionally and physically healthy children, love goes a lot further than money.

Children suffer neglect when they are not provided training for basic life skills or are denied medical care for good health, especially when that care is readily available. When parents place children in roles that are beyond their ken, such as caring for much younger children, maintaining the home, and leaving them to fend for themselves, they have neglected to care for their children.

Feelings of abandonment occur when a child is left alone for unreasonable periods of time, is forgotten about, or is left to be cared for by others rather than by the parents (without reason or explanation). When a child is not held, cuddled,

---

[50] Ed Henry, *42 Faith: The Rest of the Jackie Robinson Story*, (Nashville: Thomas Nelson, 2017), 60-61.

played with, or paid attention to often enough, a child is left to feel unimportant and unworthy of attention or love—emotional abandonment.

It is never appropriate for an adult to make a romantic gesture toward a child or ever initiate any type of sexual touch. Sexual abuse could occur with an acquaintance, parent, relative, mentor, sibling, teacher, or anyone who comes into contact with the child, including total strangers. Sexual abuse can range from inappropriate comments to rape and everything in between. It can happen at any age. I've worked with emergency medical staff who've talked about babies who've been sexually assaulted and raped.

Parents who attempt to have sexual relations with a child are deeply disturbed and most likely are reenacting a childhood trauma. Children who are not properly supervised will often have sex with other children and later feel deeply ashamed. It is normal for kids to be curious about one another, and a certain amount of exploration is natural, but when children are having sexual relations, there is a failure in their support system.

Some adults are covertly sexual toward their children, which can be abusive if it makes the child feel uncomfortable. Parents who flirt with their children, act seductively, parade around half-dressed, or are overly touchy-feely, are taking the risk of being eroticized by their child. When parents discuss their sex lives with their children, they are crossing an unhealthy line of fantasy that is misplaced on the child rather than on an age-appropriate person at an age-appropriate time. Children need to perceive their parents as wholesome adults, not sex objects.

Emotional incest occurs when a parent uses a child as a surrogate partner. The child is used as a confidant, a support person, or a substitute for the absentee parent. Expected to fill every role but having sex with the parent, the child is placed in the adult role of caretaker or partner, which creates an emotional bind where the child feels both powerful and trapped: empowered by a sense of superiority and simultaneously robbed of freedom. Adults need to share their personal lives, social interests, and adult concerns with other adults, not their kids.

Verbal abuse causes a child to feel humiliated and worthless. Name calling and raging at a child are not only belittling, but they also teach a child to yell rather than talk out angry feelings. Talking down to, using sarcasm, or criticizing a child also diminishes self-esteem. All verbal abuse is a noncreative way to communicate frustration. To use fear to enforce compliance destroys a child's desire to make good choices for the sake of feeling good.

Physical abuse can be moderate to severe, but in every case is a poor alternative to administering other consequences, such as time-out, temporary loss of a privilege, or loss of a favored object. Physical abuse occurs when a parent is too angry or too unskilled to know any different and administers force. When children are struck by the parents or hit with objects to the point of bodily harm, it is abusive. Children who are yanked can suffer dislocated shoulders. Children who are thrown can have broken bones. Children who are shaken often suffer brain damage. According to the National Center for Fatality Review and Prevention, head trauma, internal bleeding from kicks to the abdomen, burning, drowning, and suffocation are the major causes of death related to child abuse.[51]

Let us remember that the invisible hole has many opportunities to form from experiences outside of the home and by someone else who hurts the child. In many cases of sexual abuse, the perpetrator threatens to hurt the child or another family member if the child reports it. Or sometimes the abuse is reported, and the parents fail to address the issue because of their own inadequacies. Regardless of the circumstances, if the wound is not healed, it does not vanish, and it remains hidden in the unconscious. These are just some of the types of abuse that create the invisible hole.

Sometimes a patient will tell me, "It wasn't that bad, we had everything we needed, and at least I wasn't beaten or raped." My stance on this is that it doesn't matter whether you were shot in the foot or the abdomen, you suffered a trauma, and the trauma you experienced doesn't need to be compared to anyone else's. Anything that causes a child to feel like less than a lovable human being will open up the invisible hole.

Children who feel loved and cared for and are raised to trust their own perceptions and instincts transfer those experiences to the world outside and have the ability to cope with the imperfections of life.

No parent is perfect; I've made some of the worst mistakes. If you are a parent, it won't do any good to feel guilty. Children are resilient and can endure imperfect parenting. If a parenting mistake is acknowledged and corrected, children are quick to

---

[51] "Child Abuse and Neglect," The National Center for Fatality Review and Prevention, www.ncfrp.org/reporting/child-abuse-and-neglect/.

forgive, but if the parent fails to acknowledge, continues, or justifies inappropriate behavior, the wound will fester. Most of us make the same errors as our parents did, or we make new errors by overcompensating in an attempt to do the opposite. The goal is that we keep on learning with improvement. If we can do even a little bit better than our parents, each generation will do a better job at producing healthier children, free from the bondage of addiction.

Self-Evaluation Questionnaire

1. Make a chart with two sides. On one side list the components of a healthy template, including your own ideas. Circle the ones you received as a child. Next, make a list of all the components that were missing in your childhood. Underline the ones you are willing to provide for yourself now.

2. Do you feel you were micromanaged as a child? How did this affect you?

3. Were you neglected? Hungry, cold, lonely, lost? If so, describe what caused you to feel this way.

4. Were you emotionally abused? If so, how?

5. Physically abused? If so, how?

6. Sexually abused? If so, how?

7. What do you think caused your parents to raise you the way they did?

8. If you are a parent, what parenting patterns did you repeat (or are you repeating) with your children?

9. If you are a parent, how would you like to do (or have done) things differently?

CHAPTER SEVEN

THE PAIN TEMPLATE

The wound is the place where the Light enters you.
—Rumi

Addiction is like touching a hot burner over and again. You don't think you will get burned the next time, but you do. The important question to ask is, why keep touching the burner?

Becoming aware that you have been trying to fill an invisible hole is not enough to stay clear of or beat addiction. There's some work to be done first. You must come to understand how your brain has been wired with a specific template and become aware of how that template has kept you going up and down and all around the maze. Then you can start creating a new template for your future.

During early childhood, the unconscious mind operates like a computer and records everything it sees and hears. The recording forms a mental template that is permanently branded in the mind.

That template becomes an internal point of reference for adult life. It resembles the concept of the Imago that Harville

Hendrix describes in his classic, *Getting the Love You Want*. The difference is that his model focuses solely on uncovering the source of frustrations within a romantic relationship. I use the term "pain template" because I have seen in my decades-long practice that people create all kinds of relationships destined to retrigger childhood wounds from all kinds of sources.

Children who witness loving parents, have their needs met, and grow up feeling safe develop a pleasure template. Children who witness or experience abuse develop a pain template. People who were harmed as children are likely to continue to be harmed (victims) or will turn around and harm others (perpetrators), because that is their mental map for child-rearing and interpersonal relationships—it's how they were programmed.

Most people know that it is never good to be abused or be abusive, and yet many people reenact their childhood nightmares even after they had sworn they never would. The internal template veers toward the same direction, and it's impossible to change without the tools. As long as the pain template is reenacted, the wound grows and all non-therapeutic attempts to get rid of the pain only make the hole bigger. It is a vicious cycle.

Freud explains that when we are triggered by someone (positively or negatively), we are experiencing transference. Here's how transference works: If, when you were a child, your mother was hypercritical of you, that transfers to your experience now as an adult. Every time you perceive (accurately or not) someone being critical of you, you have a strong

THE PAIN TEMPLATE | 117

reaction, sometimes to the point of obsessing about it for days. I'm not talking about mild annoyances that might trigger a minor reaction that quickly evaporates like a wisp of cloud. I'm talking about a tornado that has been brewing for years—the vortex around the invisible hole. The current event has a taproot from an earlier wound that gets triggered by a similar event and causes you to feel flooded with emotion. I call it "going nuclear." You feel an extreme reaction that you can't shake off. Two common ineffective strategies people use to push it out is to blame someone else for the discomfort or kill it off through self-medicating. Either one of these strategies represents a missed opportunity to heal a wound you might have carried your entire life.

It doesn't matter which current event is triggering the reaction, if you're going nuclear, it's about the past. The event has triggered some childhood abuse or trauma and detonates the reaction. Here's an example: If your parents often kept you waiting during your childhood, you may have stood outside of the school, all by yourself, waiting and waiting, feeling more and more afraid. Now that you're an adult when someone is late, you relive that fear, and you're not even aware of why you feel so upset. By the time the person does arrive, you are so charged, you lash out or hold onto the negative energy generated by your reaction, and your friend has no idea why you are so triggered.

Every patient with whom I have ever worked demonstrated the pattern of reenacting the pain template, then attempting to medicate away the pain. Let's take Karl, who was born into a family with two teenage parents. His was an unplanned birth.

He felt his parents loved each other, but his wound started to form when weekends were frequently ruined when his parents got drunk and fought. By the time he was ten, his parents had divorced; his mother was only twenty-three, his father twenty-four. That wound formed a deeper hole when he was shuffled around to different relatives. He felt angry, confused, and abandoned. He missed having his family together, and the pain of loss and loneliness widened the invisible hole inside.

In his early teens, Karl started trying to fill his invisible hole with drugs and stole in order to support his new habit. At age sixteen, after stealing from an employer, he was arrested, but he was able to work out a plea and avoid going to jail. Karl continued to use drugs, and his life revolved around partying and his new drug of choice—sex.

At age seventeen, Karl dropped out of high school to work full time in construction. His dependence on drugs increased, and he continued to have run-ins with the law. When he was twenty-one, while at a friend's party, a young girl approached him for sex; she was fourteen (the same age as Karl's mother when he was born), and he complied. Several days later, he was arrested for having sex with a minor and later was convicted. He spent two years in jail without fully comprehending what he'd done wrong. Over the next decade after his release, he was in and out of jail on convictions of disorderly conduct and drug-related charges. During his final incarceration, he was introduced to a 12-Step program and stopped using alcohol and drugs. This was the first time he'd turned his life in a positive direction. Once sober, Karl stopped getting into trouble with the law. He began therapy because he wanted to get married, but he and his girlfriend often fought—mostly about sex.

Karl's pain template for relationships began when he saw his parents' intense fighting, followed by their divorce and the instability that ensued. The widening pain gnawed away at him, and the invisible hole that formed grew with each recurring painful event. Now that drugs and alcohol were no longer an option, he had become obsessed with using sex to medicate his wound. He wanted to have sex at least once a day, and his girlfriend felt overwhelmed by his demands.

Karl had started using at a young age, which only buried his painful memories alive and delayed his ability to mature. Like his parents, he acted out his anger by breaking the law, causing him jail time. Having two teenaged parents, Karl did not see himself as a grown man when he had sex with a teenager, and he felt he'd been blamed unjustly, further expanding his internal wound.

Once Karl recognized that he had been using drugs and sex to avoid feeling unresolved childhood pain, he had a decision to make. To break free of addiction, he would have to face the pain his addiction was covering up, heal the wound, then learn a new template for a healthy, intimate relationship, with sex being only one component. When I last met with Karl, he said he would be back in touch when he was ready to do the work. He has touched base from time to time, but he has yet to be willing to commit.

Once you are able to recognize that you can heal your reactions and be comfortable in your own body, you won't need to escape your feelings anymore. By following the steps in this book, you can learn to embrace your emotions so you won't need to self-medicate. When you perceive your emotions as a valued aid rather than your enemy, you can give yourself the power to steer away from the addictive nosedive and crash and instead stay the course to freedom.

Candy-Coated Pain

The pain template isn't always a result of an obvious trauma. Some forms of pain are inflicted in the name of love. Children who are smothered with food or care suffer this type of pain. It is important that children be allowed to experience their feelings and be taught how to release them in healthy ways. If children are sad and encouraged to cry, they will find an emotional release in expelling the pain. When angry children are taught to talk about the anger, they will not act out in destructive ways. Some parents don't like to see their children suffer and inadvertently offer the kind of help that teaches suppression, such as telling their children they should "buck up" or "don't cry; you're fine."

Joanna started therapy because she was depressed. When I first met her, her strawberry blonde hair was unruly, she was so heavy she had difficulty walking, and she seemed emotionally shut down. She had a twenty-year-old daughter, Lisa, she had raised alone. Joanna's life revolved around her medical career and food. She had been in treatment for an eating disorder and had lost weight, but she relapsed when her daughter attempted suicide.

Lisa had taken a drug overdose after she remembered being sexually assaulted by her babysitter when she was only two years old. Joanna admitted that it was true, and she was overwhelmed with guilt that she had allowed a man she barely knew to care for her child.

Joanna also had been raised by a single mom. She remembered her mother as a cold woman who only showed love through food. Whenever Joanna was sad, her mother told her, "Here, eat this; you will feel better." Food was the suggested solution for any problem. By the time Joanna entered first grade, she was so overweight the other kids made fun of her, further expanding her wound.

Her invisible hole had begun to form, and she filled this void with the only thing she knew—more food. When Joanna entered high school, her life centered on eating and making good grades. When she was finishing nursing school, Joanna was lonely and needy, so she was easily seduced when a fellow staff member showed an interest in her. Their first date ended in her first sexual experience, nonconsensual, and that was the last she heard from him.

Filled with feelings of abandonment and regret, Joanna consoled herself the same way she always had, with food. At first, she thought her weight gain was related to binging on pastries and candy, but after several months of missed periods, she discovered she was pregnant. Twenty years later and a hundred pounds heavier, the crisis with her daughter's attempted suicide propelled her to get help.

Even though Joanna's eating disorder had been treated, the invisible hole remained intact, and she continued to reenact the pain template her mother taught her: Stuff the pain that caused the wound then fill the invisible hole with food. As Joanna progressed through therapy, she regularly attended a 12-Step meeting for food addicts, and instead of eating sugar and wheat, she was able to access and release emotions bottled inside of her. She also engaged in family therapy, so Lisa could talk about her sexual abuse, and Joanna could offer her daughter the maternal support needed to heal her painful trauma.

When Pain Templates Collide

The most intriguing aspect of pain templates is how two people tend to meet and match their pain templates in such a way that perfectly reenacts both people's past wounds. We most often hear how this plays out in romantic relationships, but the pain template collision can occur in any type of relationship—parent to child, friend to friend, peer to peer.

The most common setup for a pain template collision is when a child of an addict is unconsciously drawn into an affiliation with an addict. Addicts try to fill an invisible hole that's projected through their pain template while using the other person as a human repair kit; at the same time, children of addicts are trying to fill their invisible hole by repairing the addict, so they can finally receive the love and attention they did not get as a child. Both are trying to find their way out of the maze, but they are merely reenacting the same pain template that was created in childhood. These attempts to fill the invisible hole by reenacting the childhood nightmare will only fail, unless one or both people in the relationship commit to doing the individual work that will heal the wounds that drive them.

There will never be enough of anything external to fill the invisible hole. You can have all the booze, drugs, food, power, sex, attention, and anything else you want, but all of those things are like pouring a bottle of Drano into your soul. If you want to get well, you will have to stop hurting yourself and learn how to fill the invisible hole with actions that will heal the wound. You can stop using and go to the best therapists and treatment centers, but that won't be enough if you don't address the invisible hole. The following questions will help you identify if you have a pain template and if so, how it was formed.

Self-Evaluation Questionnaire

1. Did you feel you were wanted as a child?

2. What early painful events started forming the hole? What was the most painful?

3. List any negative messages you were told that made you feel "less than."

4. How have those negative messages continued throughout your life?

5. How did you cope with painful feelings?

6. Were you forced to think or feel a certain way or were you ostracized (at home, school, a religious institution, or elsewhere)?

7. Did you ever feel you were physically hurt by a loved one (other than an accident)? What happened?

8. Was there enough to eat and enough personal care in your family? If not, what was missing?

9. Did you spend endless hours alone? Were you lonely? Did you feel at times you weren't important to your parents? If the answer to any of these is yes, write down which memories these questions bring to light.

10. Did anyone ever try to touch you in a way that felt sexually inappropriate or wrong to you? If so, what did you do?

11. Did you feel comfortable with the way your parents dressed at home (or were not dressed)? Clarify what you saw and what you felt.

12. Did anything else happen in your childhood you have had a hard time living with? If so, describe that experience now if you can.

CHAPTER EIGHT

ROMANTIC IMPRINTS

I'm not crying because of you; you're not worth it. I'm crying
because my delusion of who you were was shattered
by the truth of who you are.
—Steve Maraboli

Pain templates can be played out in any kind of relationship. But romantic relationships deserve a chapter all their own because they can be so intense. We also have the added complication of the euphoria and addictive brain chemistry that gets activated through romantic attraction and sex. Often the most intense romantic relationships begin based solely on physical attraction and quickly devolve when the hormone high starts to wear off. When there's a breakup, the sober addict is ill-equipped to cope with the intensity of withdrawal emotions and is likely to relapse. I have seen more people relapse on substances after a relationship went south than any other trigger.

The common cause for an immediate magnetic attraction is the romantic imprint. An imprint is a sensory-visual image that is branded into the mind. A romantic imprint occurs when the first blush of passion overtook you, usually around the fifth or sixth grade. Suddenly, someone stirred you in such a way that you were never the same. Your heart went pitter-patter, and you felt flushed, excited, as if you could walk on air. Everyone else paled in this person's presence. You couldn't stop thinking about the person, you had sleepless nights, and you lost your appetite. You found a part of you that had never emerged, one full of creativity, excitement, and longing.

When I tell people that they have such an imprint, they often rebuff the idea, but I invite you to let this idea marinate a little bit and see what awareness might surface. Without fail, every person who has given this notion some thought has been able to retrieve the image of that first person, whose appearance became the preferred look of any future potential partners.

We all know that first blush of puppy love is healthy and normal, but when a young person is carrying unhealed trauma that has formed into the invisible hole, the first romantic imprint can be addictive. An image of who you saw in that moment becomes stamped in the mind, and once linked to that first innocent puppy love feeling, can turn into a drug-like driving force to seek that same high.

Addiction to People

Though few ever recognize it, ever since that first crush, we have a natural tendency to be attracted to the same physical type as our imprint. A healthy, well-adapted person who is not prone to addiction is able to discern that physical attraction doesn't necessarily equate to compatibility, so they will weigh physical attraction as well as other elements of compatibility in considering a potential partner. On the other hand, a person carrying an unhealed wound who is vulnerable to addiction is way more likely to mistake the effects of a powerful physical attraction for true love.

Laura and Mike came to therapy because they wanted to stop fighting. She was tall and thin, with long black hair and green eyes; he was also tall, with brown hair and blue eyes. They were both in their mid-forties and physically fit. Laura had been practicing law for several years; Mike was a manager at a local Cadillac dealer. Neither had been married or had children.

They had met at a 12-Step social function, and from the moment they spotted one another, it was as though no one else was in the room. They were inseparable the whole evening. After leaving the meeting, they went for coffee then back to Mike's place for "wild sex." Two weeks later, Mike told Laura she was the "one" he'd been waiting for and asked her to move in with him.

This is a classic beginning of an unconscious relationship driven by a strong mutual imprint match. Things went well for the first three months, then the fighting began when they triggered each other's pain templates. Laura said Mike was moody, and Mike said Laura was a workaholic. A pattern ensued where neither attempted to understand the other, the bickering intensified to screaming, and Laura would leave the house. After several days, Mike would become heartsick and text Laura to come back. They would reunite in blissful sex. But after a few days, the pattern would start all over again.

Having worked with many people in addictive relation-ships, I understood how their pain templates had collided and how hard it was for them to break their patterns. Like many couples I've seen, by the time they came to therapy, Laura and Mike were emotionally drained.

With this couple, Mike would blame Laura for not paying enough attention to him, and Laura would call Mike a control freak. All of the empathy exercises and active listening techniques I tried to teach ended in boxing matches where words were thrown like punches.

"You didn't do your homework; you obviously don't care about me," Mike would tell Laura, and she would reply, "You're crazy. I can't do this anymore!" All of their energy went into blaming one another, leaving them with no energy for compassion or building understanding. It was clear to me that Mike and Laura had been pulled into each other's imprint, but without a foundation of trust built over time, their sexual attraction for one another was not enough for a sustainable relationship. On top of that, each had personality traits that activated the other's childhood wounds.

When their wounds collided, their pain templates were reenacted, preventing them from being present to the here and now. Unless and until they each healed the wounds that had triggered them, they would not learn how to share their pain with each other and show empathy for the other person. Even more important, they would continue to miss the opportunity to recognize that the wounds they triggered in each other could be a doorway to healing the past, if they were willing to open it. As long as they believed they were reacting to their partner, and not their past, their chance for change and growth was nil.

Laura's mother was prone to rage. She always had found fault with Laura. The oldest of five children, Laura was forced to take responsibility for her siblings and couldn't remember "just being a kid." Her sense of responsibility for her family put her in the role of a surrogate mother rather than a child. Her parents were never married, her father was absent throughout her childhood, and she never formed a relationship with him.

Mike, too, had a father who had abandoned the family when Mike was young; he was raised by his mother with whom he "never felt safe." He remembers all through his childhood feeling manipulated through guilt. He felt like he was supposed to take care of his mother rather than the reverse. He could not recall her ever paying much attention to him; it was all about her. At the car dealership, Mike was required to work long hours, and when he came home, he wanted Laura to pay attention to him. Laura's job as an attorney was stressful, and when she came home, she wanted to relax for the evening and take some time for herself. Her lack of interest in Mike set off his pain template of having had a mother who used him for her own needs, and he re-lived the painful wound of abandonment. When Mike would become angry with Laura, it triggered her pain template of her mother raging at her when she didn't jump up to tend to the kids.

Neither Mike nor Laura had parents that modeled healthy parenting or healthy adult partnership. They both had assumed the position of adult replacements for the missing parent. When triggered in their relationship as adults, they were consumed by old feelings of not being properly cared for, followed by anger and resentment. The unconscious reenactment of their dysfunctional childhood family only wore them down because they were (psychologically) living in the past rather than being able to enjoy each other in the now.

No amount of therapy could help this couple until they each were willing to recognize they were reenacting the pain templates of their childhoods: Laura's resentment of her mother's demands on her and Mike's feelings of a mother who'd emotionally abandoned him and used him to fill her own needs. Both agreed to do the work necessary to heal their individual wounds and learn how to communicate in an entirely new way. In spite of threatening to leave therapy whenever they felt uncomfortable, they managed to stick it out and keep their appointments.

Slowly, Laura and Mike began to see that they each were reacting to an unhealed past. They both worked through their old pain, but as the emotional intensity lessened, boredom set in. Mike and Laura had known only the wanton electricity of their sexual relationship, and now they had to build the circuitry of friendship and trust.

At one point, Laura made the choice to move out and continue to see Mike in couple's therapy. She realized she had never lived alone, and she wanted to learn how. At first Mike threatened to break up, but Laura communicated she did not want to break up; she wanted to build something new.

She followed through by spending time with Mike and insisting they do more activities like going out for coffee, so they could talk. As they got to know one another, they began to understand their attraction had been primarily physical, and they were not compatible. They had little in common, and the relationship had gone adrift. When Laura's firm relocated her to an office in another state, she stopped therapy, and eventually the couple parted on good terms.

Even though their relationship did not last, it was not a failure. Unlike many couples, Laura and Mike had the courage to face the internal pain the relationship had brought up, and instead of blaming, they each were able to heal. Having addressed their pain templates, they were more likely to make progressive improvement in their relationship choices in the future.

My husband, Skip, and I are an example of unmatched imprints who have successfully navigated our way into an intimate relationship. He was my imprint; I was not his. Even so, we started off as friends, and over many months, our relationship blossomed into romance as our respect and enjoyment of each other grew. Though we each came into the relationship with our individual pain templates, we had healed our wounds enough to have ventured out of the maze, and we were able to use our conflicts as the doorway to deeper growth. In our relationship, we both are able to be vulnerable, share our pasts, and gain an understanding of each other's triggers. This understanding enables us to use those triggers as an opportunity to heal another piece of the past rather than reenact old wounds. For example, I've told him, "I feel anxious when you're late and don't tell me because when I was little, I was often waiting for hours for someone to wake up and take care of me." He might tell me, "When you tell me how to do things, it reminds me of my mother's incessant control of my life." This way of communicating allows us to view each other's actions and reactions without taking them personally and to be more sensitive and aware of how we trigger one another. Through this ongoing practice, we have built a relationship that allows us to feel close, safe, and cared for.

The Addiction of Codependency

Another manifestation of addiction is known as codependency. Instead of a person being addicted to a thing or a behavior, codependency represents an addiction to another person. Sometimes a child whose parents were addicted grows up to be addicted to unhealthy people. Signs of codependency occur when one person's life revolves around another's, and all of the symptoms of addiction manifest, such as loss of control, attempt to control, needing more to get the same effect, negative consequences, loss of friends, loss of self-care, ill health, and symptoms of emotional and physical withdrawal in the face of losing the codependent connection. Addictive relationships frequently happen with couples who are romantically attracted, but in the absence of a love connection, codependency also occurs in many nonromantic relationships.

For example, parents who are codependent with their children either live vicariously through their children's success, or they take care of the child beyond a reasonable age of adulthood. Caretakers who live for another and lack a satisfying life of their own often are addicted to the person they care for, or in some cases, they are addicted to an organization or institution. Regardless of circumstance, when the codependent feels abandoned by the person (or organization) in whom they have placed their focus, the codependent will experience many if not all of the withdrawal symptoms of any other addiction.

A case in point: Melissa was referred to me by another therapist who told her she needed to grieve the loss of her son, Jess. Her world revolved around Jess, as she unsuccessfully tried to control his drug habit. Melissa did not realize that all of the fear-based things she did were not helping Jess. He started using drugs in high school and later dropped out, at which point he spent most of his time either hanging out with his drug-using friends or isolated in his room. Melissa's life was consumed with transporting him, cooking for him, and trying to meet his every need, all in the hope that he would change. She was not consciously aware that she was using her son as a substitute for a relationship with another adult.

After his first overdose, Jess completed a thirty-day treatment program then returned home. In spite of his therapist's urging, Melissa did not participate in his treatment and did not attend Al-Anon meetings because she felt "uncomfortable." Fearful her son would not get well without her, Melissa continued to manage his life, cooking and cleaning for him and supporting him financially. Jess did not attend recovery meetings, and with no sober friends or tools, he resumed his drug habit shortly after he came home. Tragically, a month after his return, Melissa found Jess unconscious in his bed. When the EMTs arrived, they were unable to resuscitate him, and he was pronounced dead at the scene.

When I asked about her feelings, Melissa changed the subject and started talking about her sister, the new subject of

Melissa's care. She complained that her sister was "ordering" her around, and she did not have any free time for herself. She'd switched her codependency addiction from her son to her sister.

When I pointed out that she must be in shock, Melissa skipped over my inquiry and complained her sister was putting too much responsibility on her. I was struck by the fact that Melissa was unable to feel her suffering and functioned as if she were on autopilot, going through robotic motions. She told me her childhood had been awful but could not elaborate other than by stating that she never felt safe growing up. Any attempts to draw out her feelings were unsuccessful. Melissa canceled her second appointment, stating her sister had told her they needed to help their parents, and there wasn't enough money for therapy, which was the opposite of what she'd said initially—that she was ready to start investing in herself.

Melissa had set up her life so it always rotated around another person's wants and needs, which, like any other manifestation of addiction, served as a distraction from her true feelings. She thought she was helping others, but her actions didn't take into account the genuine needs of others or herself. Her caretaking had a secondary gain of keeping her emotionally numb while attempting to cover up the invisible hole left by a lifetime of pain.

Many people think that therapy is some type of magical quick fix to a long-term problem. Even the best of therapists cannot help a patient who is unwilling to do the work. More often than not, patients use a therapist as a sounding board, but when it's time to go deeper and heal the wound, they opt out.

When I first meet with a patient, we agree to a treatment plan that includes frequency of visits as well as home assignments. I would say roughly two or three out of a hundred patients actually do the exercises. When it comes time to take a deeper look at the pain template so it can be healed, a great deal of resistance shows up.

Some work through it, but most don't. Addicts use their addiction to distract themselves from the feelings they have avoided their whole lives. Acting out the wound is dramatic, but it is also familiar. While it distracts from the real pain, it keeps the wound alive rather than felt. Even though this is counterproductive to healing, the familiarity of being sucked into the drama provides temporary relief from facing the wound, which feels scary and uncomfortable.

Locked in Love

Sometimes we confuse love with pain. If you measure feelings of love by how much pain you're in, your brand of love is more about codependency than love. Every addiction represents an unhealed wound from your past, including codependent addiction to people or institutions. Ideally, your relationships form an interdependent connection based on supporting one another rather than on making demands for unmet childhood needs.

Codependency and love addiction are the two ways people reenact their original childhood wounds and substitute addiction to a person for genuine love. Unlike genuine love, codependency has a hidden agenda of, "What can you do for me, and what do I have to do to get that?"

When you love yourself, you have no need to search for someone to take care of your needs or to complete you. You are able to decide whether or not to be together based on how good you are for one another and how well you can complement each other's needs. When you share love with another, you wish for the other person everything you wish for yourself, including the freedom to leave. When people confuse pain with love, they often become addicted to the pain, mistaking it for love. To lose someone is painful and temporary; refusal to let go is ongoing torture.

Strangely enough, for the love addict, the pain seems to be a preferable alternative to the temporary void of a breakup. When a loss or the threat of a loss occurs, the pain that follows convinces an addict that love is causing that pain. Love, including self-love, has no pain because love knows no lack. It is complete unto itself and needs nothing. The addiction is ever-present to remind us of lack, and it tells us we must fear a loss because this love affair, friendship, or work connection will never be replaced. When we operate from such fear, we hang onto people long after they no longer need to be a part of our lives.

We must remember that all addictions are an expression of the same condition: an attempt to escape the feelings of emptiness and the vortex of pain around the invisible hole. Until an addicted person faces that pain and emptiness and heals it, life will be like a circus where the addict takes the precarious swing from one trapeze to the next without a net.

Having read all this, if you see that you have been caught in the addiction maze, know that you do not have to stay in the maze any longer. There is a way out, and it's much quicker than you think. The question is: Are you willing to do what it takes to heal?

Put another way: Do you want to spend a lifetime of being disconnected from your true self and purpose, or are you willing to undergo the psychic surgery that will restore your true identity? If you choose to remain disconnected, know that you are choosing a sentence of life imprisonment where you will never escape the pain. You will only cover it up for brief, fleeting moments, while you brew up more internal turmoil. The journey to healing will feel worse at first, as it will require you to delve deep down into the vortex of the original pain you suffered as a child, but as your wound heals, you will be lifted out of the maze.

The first step is to decide that you want to get out of the maze; the decision must be made by you, for you, and not for anyone else but you.

I invite you to imagine your life as you dreamt it before you stopped dreaming. Visualize a life of joy, free of addiction and its impact. Picture yourself waking up feeling excited about what the day has to offer. It's never too late to recapture the part of you that was born to have a life of meaning and purpose—with loving relationships, a career or other work about which you are passionate, and the ability to ride life's ups and downs. This life waits for you to embrace it, but first you need to see where you are.

The following questions will help you determine if you are in a maze of addiction.

Self-Evaluation Questionnaire

1. Do you feel that you are in a maze? If so, draw what your maze looks like, identifying each corridor you have traveled that has kept you in the maze. Write in the center of the maze the wounds that have fueled the vortex and formed the hole.

2. Are you willing to get out of the maze? If the answer is yes, start your journey now by answering the rest of the questions.

3. Describe the pattern that has kept you trapped. Or going back to the same addiction. Or kept you from trying a new path.

4. List all your habits that you feel have gotten out of control.

5. How did you know you were out of control?

6. Describe your first crush: What color hair, eyes, height, shape, etc., have stuck in your mind? Describe the feelings of the first crush. Where did you feel it in your body? Did your face turn red? Were you nervous? Was your heart racing? Did you feel sexually aroused?

7. Have you carried that imprint forward in your romantic life? List the partner(s) you recall who match that original imprint.

8. Were you compatible with that imprint? Why or why not?

9. What areas of compatibility are the most important to you?

10. With whom was your most successful relationship? What made it that way?

PART III

ONE CURE

Many experts believe that an addiction can't be cured; it can only be stopped. Merriam-Webster's dictionary defines a cure as "recovery or relief from a disease." If an addiction is an illness, or "disorder" as the DSM claims, it seems to me that "recovery or relief" from that condition would be a cure. Following that train of thought, it would also seem that when someone stops engaging in an addiction, the cure would be automatic, but we know this is not the case. Once people become addicted, they can never safely resume that behavior no matter the length of abstinence.

We do not fully understand why someone who has become addicted can never safely resume that particular activity, but we do know that addicted people have lost the ability to predict what will happen when they reengage. The unfortunate proof of this fact can be seen in the millions of people who have repeatedly tried to manage an addiction with occasional indulgence and have failed. Even those people who, after decades of abstinence, reengaged in the addictive behavior ultimately come to find that they were as badly addicted or worse than before they quit. Even those who've had years of therapy and thought they were safe to dabble found out otherwise. Perhaps the cause is permanent brain change that science has failed to fully understand. Whether we use medical or psychological reasoning, we need to accept the fact that, once "recovered," addicts can never safely partake of the thing to which they were addicted. A cure for addiction requires more than abstinence. My goal here is not to analyze why we cannot reverse an addiction. My goal is to show you a path beyond mere abstinence that leads straight to permanent remission— a cure.

CHAPTER NINE

LOVE IS THE ONLY CURE

The greatest disease in the West today is not TB or leprosy; it is being unwanted, unloved, and uncared for. ... There are many in the world who are dying for a piece of bread but there are many more dying for a little love.

—Mother Teresa

People who love themselves don't want to self-destruct. When we understand this basic concept, addiction can be eradicated before it ever starts. If the billions of dollars thrown at fighting addiction could be turned into teaching the value of self-love starting with parenting, the invisible hole would never form in the first place. But for those people already suffering from addiction, the cure is the same as the prevention—love.

For our purposes, let's follow the definition that an illness (addiction) is cured as long as the person is asymptomatic. Along these lines, an addiction is no different than any other illness. Take cancer, for example; if a person is diagnosed and treated and is free of symptoms, that illness is in remission. You can remove a cancerous tumor from the lung of a smoker, but if the person continues to smoke, the "cure" probably will reverse itself, and the cancer is likely to return. But if that person never smokes again and never encounters another bout with cancer, the person remains asymptomatic, and a full remission has occurred. By definition (relieved of symptoms), that person is cured.

Concerning addiction, the glitch here is that you might be in remission without the cure, unless all of your symptoms have been treated and are gone. Just because a person isn't using doesn't mean the person is in recovery from addiction. Engaging in any addictive behavior is only one component of the illness. If you are to get well, you must treat all of the symptoms. The most important (and most often ignored) of all of the symptoms is the emotional component—the source, the pain that triggers the using. The mental obsession that creates each and every relapse is driven by the invisible hole.

Until the emotional wound is tended to and healed, no one is cured. Even if the behavior stops, the danger of relapse looms, and whenever someone or something bumps up against that wound, the trigger will set off the urge to self-medicate the pain.

A case in point: Marshall went to A.A. because his wife was concerned about his drinking. It wasn't enough that during the previous five years, he had been arrested for DUI, had lost two clients, and had an employee who quit, all because of his drinking. His denial about being addicted allowed him to compartmentalize those disasters in his mind as if they were separate, unrelated occurrences. Like any person who is addicted, he was convinced he could manage his alcohol intake. He was physically fit, handsome, and well liked in the community. In spite of the problems his alcohol use had created, Marshall managed to recover from these setbacks and bounced back. He also had managed to earn his license as an insurance agent and achieve financial success. All these things kept his denial intact. Finally, after another DUI, his wife threatened to leave if he didn't get help. Given the choice of alcohol or his marriage, but only halfway convinced he had a problem, he reluctantly went to A.A.

He stopped drinking, but his underlying wound remained. No longer able to lose himself in alcohol, he grew moody as he missed his nightly one or two bottles of wine. Marshall's wife was displeased with her (unhappy) sober husband and began to keep her distance. Thinking that giving up alcohol had been bad for him and his marriage, he resumed drinking, and within months, found himself divorced and alone—but not for long.

Marshall's sex appeal rapidly yielded a new relationship, and he continued to go on and off the wagon, reenacting the same pattern as with his wife. When his girlfriend threatened to break up with him, he would stop, then after a few months, he'd start again. At one point, Marshall's drinking became so bad, he landed in the hospital. This was his turning point. If he was to stay alive, he needed to stay sober, and to do that, he had to identify his wound and heal the pain template that propelled his self-destructive drinking.

Marshall had grown up an only child whose parents spent little time with him. He acknowledged that there was stability in his household, but he had few memories of warmth and family interaction. He recalled spending many hours alone in his bedroom, consumed with loneliness and a sense that he wasn't worth much to his parents. His low self-esteem made it difficult for him to make friends. His feeling that he was somehow defective followed him to college, where he drank alcohol for the first time, and all his insecurities seemed magically to evaporate. While drinking, he felt confident and connected. Though he was mostly a social drinker, his new best friend, alcohol, never let him down: He joined a fraternity, got a girlfriend, and created a life he could call his own.

During the next thirty years, his elixir friend turned into his silent enemy, as it slowly hijacked his mind. By age fifty, Marshall had a choice to make: either face that demon or allow it to claim his life. Marshall's wound was clear. Ever since college, whenever the unconscious feelings of loneliness or inferiority crept up on him, he drank. Abstinence offered sobriety, but not relief. Each time the pain hit a certain threshold, he sought comfort in his addiction.

Anytime he felt a loved one pull away, he experienced overwhelming feelings of abandonment. When his wife had been distant, he became flooded with the old feelings of loneliness that he had endured throughout his childhood. Once Marshall stopped using alcohol, he found himself still stuck in the same teenage state of mental isolation he'd experienced before he started drinking. Once again, Marshall felt unable to make new friends, engage in new hobbies, or otherwise take care of himself by meeting his needs in healthy ways.

After his divorce, the same pattern continued with his girlfriend, as any perceived distance on her part triggered him again. The first glass of wine obliterated the void he felt within. He felt a brief sense of relief, but once the alcohol got into his system, it once again hijacked his mind, and he lost the ability to stop. Until he addressed the core cause of his pain, he would be governed by that relentless force that would precede his first drink.

During his last binge, Marshall had become so addicted to alcohol, he could not stop drinking long enough to leave his apartment. He drank until he passed out at night, woke up with the shakes, and had to pour himself another drink to function. His drinking had gone the full progression, from anxiety relief, to negative consequences, to complete physical addiction and withdrawal. Fortunately, at this point Marshall called someone he'd met in A.A. and asked for help. Marshall became open to the possibility that something deep within him needed to be addressed, and he agreed to return to A.A. meetings. He also agreed to therapy, so he could excavate and heal the wounds of his past that continued to drive his addiction.

During the next year, Marshall was able to stay sober while he ventured into the invisible hole and properly grieved. With each healed memory, he filled the invisible hole with self-love, and he grew closer to himself and those around him.

It's been five years since Marshall had his last drink. He's gone on to live a full life, enjoying a rewarding career, friendships, golf, and travel. The last time I saw Marshall, he told me he wouldn't drink again even if he could.

"The thought of putting alcohol in my body doesn't appeal to me anymore; it poisoned me to the point it almost killed me. Strange. Until I realized I drank for sorrow rather than pleasure, I was never going to get better. Once I dealt with all the sadness I'd ignored, there was never a good enough reason to pick up the first drink." From that point forward, Marshall's reactions were no longer rooted in his past, and as long as he continues to take care of himself, Marshall can consider himself cured from alcoholism.

Another patient, Elaine, came to therapy for severe depression. She'd been diagnosed with breast cancer and had undergone a mastectomy and chemotherapy. She was in remission, but the life-threatening experience had opened the floodgates of pain that she'd carried with her since early childhood. When she came to therapy, she told me that she wanted to die, but she could not kill herself because she feared her children would be devastated.

When Elaine was five, she'd been told by her father that she was the result of an unplanned pregnancy; shortly thereafter, he died. Elaine adopted the belief that somehow her being born had caused his death. Unable to assuage her own guilt, she could not mourn her father's death. Her guilty feelings and sense of being unwanted were compounded when her mother had to work long hours to pay the bills, and she and her two siblings were left to care for themselves. Several times during her childhood, Elaine had been sent to stay with an aunt who was cold toward her and with whom she did not feel welcomed.

Her aunt, deeply involved in her church, brought Elaine to services several times each week where she was instructed to adhere to Old Testament principles or face the wrath of God. Elaine's aunt homeschooled her through junior high and high school. At age eighteen, she married a man she'd met at church, and they had three children. Overwhelmed with childcare, unhappy in her marriage, and feeling under the control of an oppressive deity, Elaine hoarded candy bars and chocolate that she would binge on when her family was asleep. Eating became her way to cope.

Elaine's life was spent in silent suffering as she rotated her world around family and church, neither of which she felt she ever freely chose; they had been imposed on her by an aunt who wanted to be freed from the responsibility of caring for Elaine. It wasn't until she faced a medical crisis with breast cancer at age fifty that a lifetime of pent-up pain and frustration descended upon her.

Even though Elaine had survived successful surgery and treatment, she fell into a deep depression. Food and her grown children were her only remaining pleasures to soothe her pain template. Since all of her children lived out of town, Elaine was left to turn mostly to food. Elaine lived to eat, and her husband made sure she was well fed, ordering pizza, soda, ice cream, and all of their other favorite comfort foods—their only remaining connection.

Elaine felt trapped. She did not want to remain married to a man she did not love, but she would not allow herself to think of an alternative without reliving the same guilt she felt for believing she'd killed her father. She now believed getting cancer was a punishment from God for that imaginary sin of killing her father.

As part of her therapy, she begrudgingly agreed to go to 12-Step meetings to address her food addiction. She began to meet new friends outside of her current life, and she found a connection to a higher power that made sense to her—with a loving God, not a wrathful one. As her depression slowly lifted and her fear of being punished subsided, Elaine became ready to do the deeper work that would free her from the pain that was still driving her eating disorder and guilt.

As she moved through the layers of childhood grief at the center of her pain vortex, she began to see how her feelings of guilt over her father's death had caused her to feel unworthy. Free of guilt, she was able to grieve the loss of her father and the absence of a childhood with a unified family. Once the pain of her past left her, the need to medicate her grief with food subsided. Six months into therapy, Elaine had lost weight, was reengaged with life, and had removed the cloak of shame that forced her to stay with a man with whom she no longer wished to live. Sharing her true feelings for the first time, Elaine was able to feel love for herself and her husband without it having to be romantic. Elaine's honesty with herself, and later her husband, enabled them to form an authentic connection. Her husband began to understand Elaine's suffering and was able to let her go. They remained close friends even after their separation.

Healing Takes Courage

You might be thinking that one or both of these cases sounds too good to be true, and you might doubt that either person could break lifelong habits so easily. You should. I want you to know that it wasn't easy for either one of them. In fact, both people, and all of the others who've gotten out of the maze, had to muster all of their strength and brave their way into the vortex of unresolved pain that kept the invisible hole an open wound. As inner work or therapy brings you closer to the originating wound that formed the invisible hole in the first place, the tendency of most people is to hesitate, and many turn back.

If you want to be released from the prison of addiction and get out of the maze forever, you can, but you've got to be willing to confront the unresolved trauma and pain that caused the invisible hole to form. I am going to guide you through the process step by step. But before we do that, there are some ground rules.

The first step to choosing love over fear is to decide to stop doing hateful things to yourself (addictive behavior) and to commit to choosing love over fear when the opportunity presents itself. Choosing love over fear means giving up the illusion that you won't enjoy your life without your addiction. Loving yourself means you stop whatever is making you sicker no matter how much you've been brainwashed into thinking that you enjoy that particular thing. You will make yourself remember how awful your first taste of alcohol or tobacco was, how you felt when you lost gambling, the guilt associated with violating your own moral and sexual standards, the exhaustion you felt from working too hard, or how sick you felt from eating too much sugar. Consider the possibility that you do not enjoy something that is destroying you and your self-esteem and harming those around you. Ask yourself honestly whether a few moments of pleasure are worth the price you pay for that brief escape.

Loving yourself means caring for yourself in a way that honors your mind, body, and spirit, which means caring for your mental, physical, and spiritual health. It might take a little while to notice the shift, but once you stop engaging in self-destructive behaviors and replace them with healthy ones, you will begin to see what you've been missing. You will begin to understand what healthy love looks like and feels like.

Second, to choose love over fear means you will keep taking care of yourself no matter what—no matter how bad you feel, no matter what discomfort you need to endure, no matter how many times you fail—you will keep on practicing loving yourself and never give up. Never.

You see, nothing will ever help you if you are not willing to learn how to love yourself. The only true replacement for addiction is to learn self-love. Rather than "treating" yourself with ice cream or wine, you can learn to relish truly loving behaviors, such as being gentle with yourself, eating healthy, getting enough sleep, balancing time with others and time alone, and other reparative acts.

Love is the only thing that will give you the courage to revisit the pain that perpetuates the invisible hole and to stay there until you heal the emotional wound(s) and the pain is gone. Once that wound is healed and you replace it with self-love, the thought of destroying yourself with addictive behavior or any unloving act will no longer hold an allure.

There is only one cure for addiction, one way out of the maze, and that is you, loving yourself. Maybe, like so many of us, you don't yet know what true love feels like because your pain template taught you otherwise. You may be afraid to investigate your past and the point where addiction took hold. You don't have to worry about being hurt again by your past; it's over. The only important thing for you to do now is to learn to love yourself, and the first step is to honor yourself by choosing love over fear.

CHAPTER TEN

CHOOSE LOVE OVER FEAR

Perfect love casts out fear. If fear exists, then there is
not perfect love.

—*A Course in Miracles*

When I was newly sober, I embarked on a hard-core search for a spiritual connection that I'd always longed for but had never cultivated. I'd always enjoyed going to church, but I couldn't fully surrender there no matter how many attempts I made. I felt traditional religion promoted fear over love, and I just couldn't buy into something my intuition told me was incorrect. I'd read the Bible and thought if God, our creator, was love, how could we all be evil sinners who need to be punished? And if the primary instruction, going as far back as Moses, was to love God and to treat one another well, and it was later reinforced by Jesus to love God, love one another, and love ourselves, how did religion take us so far off track? Since when did guidance on how to live a life of respect for our creator, parents, spouse, and neighbors degrade to institutionalized shame and guilt over human frailty?

One day, while sharing these thoughts over a cup of coffee with a friend, she told me I'd probably like *A Course in Miracles.* She hadn't studied it herself, but from what she knew, she thought it might be a solution for me, and she let me know that I could get a copy at the local Unity Church. The next day, as I thumbed through the pages of the *Course*—the most compelling book I'd ever held—all I could think was, *yes, yes, yes.* I took to it like a jump in a swimming pool on a hot summer's day, and though my spiritual quest has taken me the world over, in my mind, nothing has come close to what I learned in this book.

A Course in Miracles was first put on paper by Dr. Helen Schucman, a professor of medical psychology at the Columbia-Presbyterian Medical Center in New York City. Troubled by the overwhelming conflicts in her department, she and her colleague, Dr. William Thetford, agreed that there must be a better way of addressing conflicts and differences among the staff. Shortly thereafter, Schucman, was guided by an inner voice that told her to "take notes." Questioning her own sanity, she consulted with Dr.Thetford, who encouraged her to follow through with the internal request. The resulting work was *A Course in Miracles.*

The *Course* includes a text, 365 daily exercises, and a teacher's manual. Thetford assisted Schucman's transcription, and later, a fellow psychoanalyst, Dr. Kenneth Wapnick, facilitated editing and publication by The Foundation for Inner Peace.

According to the *Course*, a miracle is defined as "a change in perception," the decision to look at a situation through the lens of love rather than fear. Given the chaos in which Schucman found herself during the writing, and the current global political polarization as I write this, we could all use some miracle-minded thinking.

Before I go on, I'd like to take a moment to clarify something important. Many people confuse *A Course in Miracles* with Marianne Williamson, mistaking her as the author. Williamson is not the author; she is a student of the *Course*, who has received national recognition through her lectures and *Course*-related books.

I have found the teachings of the *Course* have brought immeasurable healing to me and to my relationships, with greater freedom from blame, more forgiveness and vulnerability through love, and the increased ability to transcend my fears. I credit my (mostly) constant state of happiness and joy to the many hours of therapeutic healing and spiritual connection *A Course in Miracles* has provided me.

In my opinion, Gandhi, Martin Luther King, and Mother Teresa each provide an excellent example of people who have impacted the world through love. Though they were not *Course* students, they exemplify what it teaches. They spoke for unity without attacking their oppressors. Their messages inspired rather than condemned. These individuals created massive change through being what they taught, through inspiration rather than fear. This is the vital message of *A Course in Miracles*. It encourages us to look beyond the flaws of every human and to recognize that within every person is perfect love. While human flaws are apparent, we can appeal to the divine aspect in each person. When we live this way, there is no need to attack.

A Course in Miracles is a psychological/spiritual course that, in my opinion, refines psychoanalytic concepts while also renewing the teachings of Jesus to connect inwardly with God rather than placing reliance on a religious institution. Keep in mind, Helen Schucman was a psychologist, educated in psychoanalysis, and an atheist without a religious agenda. This combination made her an exceptional candidate for channeling the *Course*'s psychological contents without having a religious-based mental block on the spiritual concepts.

The *Course* teaches that within every human is a deeper consciousness, the "Holy Spirit," and it defines human consciousness as the "ego." The Holy Spirit is based in love; the ego is fear-based and keeps us stuck in a non-loving mindset toward ourselves and others.

The *Course*'s definition of ego is different from what psychologists refer to as ego, which is the healthy sense of self that is developed from being raised in an adequate environment. The *Course*'s ego definition also isn't referencing the ego that Freud introduced as a modulator between impulses and drives (the id) and an overly moral conscience (superego). If anything, the *Course*'s reference to ego would combine Freud's descriptions of id and superego as one conflicted whirl of chaos—an id that wants immediate gratification and a superego that then shames you for indulging.

The *Course*'s definition of ego is one that forms out of a painful environment. As we've previously covered, when children's needs are met, they view the world as a satisfying place of fulfillment. But when there is unresolved trauma and abuse, the child's perception of family and relationships is pain. This pain template is transferred beyond the family and projected onto the grown child's expectations in the world.

When this happens, the child's damaged ego seeks only to escape pain and find substitutes for love. This is the precursor for addiction. Since addiction at its core is a substitute for love, it's clear why love is the only cure. The Holy Spirit is the aspect of us that is not physical but eternal and one with the creator. Rather than God being some force that cannot be touched and felt, the *Course* teaches us that the Holy Spirit is the pipeline to God. As we practice listening to and following the inner guidance of that loving voice, we begin to see our lives change for the better. With time, a sense of trust and self-love grow from having that conscious contact with this innate spiritual part of ourselves.

The purpose of *A Course in Miracles* is to teach us how to choose love (listen to the Holy Spirit) over fear (heeding the whims of the ego). I realize that some people take issue with the words such as "God" and "Spirit," so if you don't like those terms, use the word "love." It is just as easy to listen to the loving voice inside of you as to anything else you'd want to call this aspect.

While this might be a new concept to you, the *Course* would say you already know everything that it offers; you have simply forgotten it because you've been taught otherwise. The *Course* explains that throughout life, your fearful ego was conditioned by an unsafe environment. You were rewarded for "good" behavior and punished for "bad" behavior. Children raised this way learn that a person can be lovable only if they follow all of the rules—a concept quite different than teaching a child they are lovable no matter what, and that loving acts bring forth good feelings, and unloving behaviors lower self-esteem. Teaching children to make decisions based on loving themselves and others requires a conscious effort on the part of role models; it's not as expedient as negative reinforcement or punishment, but it is one that yields many long-term rewards.

Good person vs. bad person is a maneuver some religions use to teach people to stop "sinning" so they can stay out of hell. The *Course* teaches us that we are already in hell when we are governed by the ego. Remember, according to the *Course's* definition, the primary purpose of the ego is to separate us from love, so we become so miserable that we make choices that take us toward death over life. The Holy Spirit teaches us how to love ourselves and how to share love with and receive love from others. When we do this, like the rats in the "Rat Park" experiment, we are too busy enjoying our lives to be consumed with addiction.

The *Course* teaches that even though the ego governs by fear, the fear is hidden behind guilt and anger. Anger pushes people away. Guilt and shame make people feel bad for what they do, but they rarely change a person's behavior. Addicts keep using whether or not they feel guilty or ashamed. I'd also like to add that the *Course* does not specifically address anxiety. I believe that anxiety is just another word for fear. When patients start labeling their "anxiety" as fear, they begin to get a new sense of personal power by walking through the fear as opposed to learning how to "manage" anxiety.

The *Course* is not referring to a healthy conscience that tells us right from wrong, but to guilt, which keeps us stuck in an unloving mindset toward ourselves as less than or unworthy, and we don't change a thing. Nor does the *Course* teach anger is bad; it simply reminds us it's a cover-up for fear. When someone is violating you or your rights, feeling angry is natural and appropriate, and when we love ourselves, we don't allow people to walk all over us. Honestly yet kindly expressing yourself to others is choosing love and not the same thing a acting out anger in an abusive manner. Though it takes more courage to gather yourself in a calm and timely manner, you can (and must) stick up for yourself without telling someone off.

Misplaced or poorly managed anger due to the ego-based fear of rejection or confrontation means that conflicts are approached through either direct or indirect attacks. Getting even (passive-aggression), secretly doing the same behavior, and bad-mouthing people behind their backs but never bringing your concerns to them directly are examples of indirect attacks.

Outright blame and verbal abuse are two examples of direct attacks. Both are equally unloving, both toward yourself and others. The *Course* points out that when acting out in anger, rather than dealing with the fear underneath anger and guilt, we project it onto another person. When we learn to ask ourselves what we fear rather than what we feel angry or guilty about, we change the course of our lives. Such an inquiry restores our inner power and allows us to face the unconscious fear that has been driving us. Then we are able to provide ourselves the loving parenting we needed as children but didn't receive enough of or in the right way, and we can walk ourselves through our emotional blocks.

When making life decisions, to which voice will you listen? Love (Holy Spirit) or fear (ego)? As I'm writing this book, I hear both voices. My ego constantly tells me that I'm opening myself up to public humiliation. I imagine every embarrassing moment of my life being aired in living color for the world to see. The other voice tells me not to worry about all that; the only thing I need to focus on is helping others, not concerning myself with made-up fears. If stories of my past can be used to help others out of the maze, then so be it.

When we love ourselves, we can learn how to make our way out of any hellhole and into a life of joy.

We are not expected to digest the *Course* teachings overnight, as they are a whole new way of thinking. When I teach the *Course*, I tell students to think of it as learning a new language; it takes time and practice. You cannot pick up a French book and speak fluent French on your first try. You need guidance and practice, and the more you work with it, the faster you learn.

On the following pages, I'm going to lead you through the steps that have healed many people of their addiction. Please keep in mind that you are not being graded, and it's OK to make mistakes. What matters is your effort, not the results, because eventually your efforts will produce positive results. I've never seen anyone go from living a life of addiction to a life of self-love overnight. Expect it to take time, keep practicing, and be patient. Each time you choose love over fear, you are tending to a long-ignored wound, and given enough time, you can heal it.

As you practice choosing love over fear, you can begin to realize the difference between treating yourself with love and abusing yourself with addiction. Just because your childhood formed a pain template doesn't mean you have to keep associating pain with pleasure. Even though the ego tells you that by indulging in your addiction, you are treating yourself to some type of reward, try to remember that your so-called "treat" is a substitute for authentic love and a poor one at that. Addiction is taking much more from you than the temporary fix it offers. Each time you get that one hit, you pay a painful price in degraded self-esteem, as well as in your power to choose, your money, your loved ones, your health, and ultimately your life.

A Course in Miracles teaches us that the ego's goal is death, and the Holy Spirit's goal is a joyful life. This is almost identical to Freud's description of Thanatos (the God of death), every person's death wish, and Eros (the God of love), every person's wish for love. Through his work treating trauma, Freud wanted us to understand there is a part of the mind that has a death instinct and a life instinct that work in opposition to one another, and that each instinct is driven by sex and aggression. It is beyond the scope of this book to elaborate on Freud's theories other than to explain that these competing drives often collide, and aggression can be turned inward resulting in depression and suicidal behavior.

As you go through the following recommendations, be aware of the natural human (ego) tendency to ignore or resist the tools that are offered to help you heal your wounds. Remember that the ego wants you to separate from life, and it uses addiction as a weapon against you. Think about it—the more you engage in an addiction, the more isolated you become. The more you withdraw, the more you feel the invisible hole, and the more you crave the addiction. The vicious cycle pulls you further into the vortex, making it harder and harder to get out.

As you become more connected to your body and the spiritual aspect of your mind, you can come to see that any form of abuse, from yourself or others, has lost its allure. The more you relate to yourself with love (from the Holy Spirit), the less that fear will have a hold on you. You will begin to see the insanity of listening to your ego when it tells you to do something self-destructive—and it will lose its grip on you.

As you proceed further into your healing, notice how your addiction and the ego work in tandem: The ego will try to convince you it's OK to do something, saying, "Lighten up. Go ahead and have another drink, eat more ice cream, have another affair, place another bet; you deserve this." But the minute the high is over and the consequences hit you, the ego rapidly condemns you for doing the very thing it convinced you to do, asking, "Why did you do that, you stupid idiot? When will you learn?!" This is how the ego keeps you in the maze and blocks you from seeing that you are addicted. It keeps convincing you that you can fill the invisible hole with things that only dig it deeper. The first time you are able to tell that voice no and give yourself love instead, you will have begun the miraculous journey of being cured of addiction.

Love Requires Action

Whether you like it or not, if you want positive results, you must decide to love yourself. Love is not just a feeling. It is an action. Let love in. Let love cast out your fear and anything else that has blocked you from loving yourself. Don't give up; even if you doubt that you're getting better, know that you are. Pretend you are in the gym of spirituality. You can look in the mirror after many workouts and not see the change, but after a month or two, your clothes fit more loosely, you're toned, and your skin has a healthy glow. Spend as much time in loving yourself as you did in your addiction, and you will get rapid results.

You may think that indulging in an addiction is being nice to yourself. It's not. Most addicted patients tell me that right before they partook, they told themselves they "deserved" to do whatever it was they weren't "supposed to do." Many addicts have used their addiction as a reward for withstanding stress or emotional pain or for achieving a goal. But what the addict does not realize is that in that moment of deciding to use, the so-called reward is actually punishment in disguise. Anyone can prove this to themselves by asking a few simple questions: Is this thing I'm about to do actually good for me? What happened the last five times I did this? Did I feel better or worse after the pleasure wore off?

Dousing any form of discontent in alcohol will never make it go away. And drowning a celebration in booze never made the achievement greater either. I want to reiterate a point made earlier, that addiction gives us the illusion that we feel good, all the while widening the invisible hole with more regret and suffering, fueling the vortex, and burying ourselves alive.

Every addictive behavior is a choice of fear over love. Hard to believe? Consider—what's the first thing that crosses your mind when you want to engage in your addiction? Doesn't the thought (from the ego) occur to you that if you don't partake, you won't like the way you feel? Isn't that fear of not feeling OK without your vice, the very thing that tells you to go ahead regardless of the consequences? Isn't that fear that you won't enjoy your life without the very thing that is killing you? If you think your addiction's temporary high is offering you anything other than short-term relief in exchange for long-term emotional and physical suffering, you are definitely on the road to death, not life.

Addictions are false substitutes for authentic love. When I tried to stop smoking for the umpteenth time, one of the healers from whom I sought help asked me why it was so hard for me to stop. "Because I love cigarettes; they have been my best friend ever since I was twelve years old." She compassionately looked into my eyes and replied, "When you can say you love yourself as much as you love cigarettes, you won't want to poison yourself anymore."

Once that thought took hold, I was free from smoking, but it didn't take long for the hole inside of me to look for another place to fill up. I started long-distance bicycling then running, thinking they were good for me, but I later realized the endorphins I obtained from the intensive exercise were the real reason I was running marathons—just another way to fill the same invisible hole. My quest for love's substitutes continued for many years. Until I realized there was nothing outside of me that could ever offer the fulfillment I sought, I was only exchanging one addiction for another.

As *A Course in Miracles* so clearly stated, I would "seek but never find." The *Course* taught me that I had not found the peace I had so desperately sought because it wasn't out there; it was within me.

Underneath every addiction is a desire to replace an unwanted feeling with a better one. The only problem is, it doesn't work. We reach for something, and sure enough, we get that momentary relief, but it quickly fades into remorse. When the addiction stops, the good feeling of being alive can return.

Remember: Until your brain is rerouted toward love, you will continue to unconsciously fear the feelings that will come up when you make the choice for abstinence. *If I don't do this, I will feel worse than I do now* is the underlying thought that precedes using. The thought of deprivation or loss is what will propel you to keep doing the very thing that creates more suffering and more loss. Like the rats in the experiment we discussed earlier, when we are addicted, we push the lever to get the quick hit without realizing that the more we push that lever, the more we actually lose. When we are addicted, we run on autopilot deeper into the maze, with our minds following the navigation of the ego telling us we ought to do something that isn't good for us. We never stop to question it.

You don't have to do this anymore. There is a way out.

The following questions are here to help you to identify whether you are guided by love or fear.

Self-Evaluation Questionnaire

1. How would you define love?

2. How would you define fear?

3. Has guilt governed you? What are some of the things you feel guilty about? Has your guilt permanently stopped you from breaking free of an unwanted pattern?

4. When you feel angry, what do you do? Shut down? Yell? How do you feel after you have either stuffed or blasted your anger?

5. Give some examples of how you have chosen fear over love.

6. Does the thought of love scare you? If so, why?

7. What are five ways you can show yourself love now?

CHAPTER ELEVEN

THREE STEPS TOWARD LOVE

Pain is inevitable. Suffering is optional.
—Haruki Murakami

Feelings are at the root of every addiction. In this chapter, we are going to confront, address, and forgive years of pent-up feelings and unaddressed pain, and you will read about ways to embrace your feelings and express them. It can be confusing to hear that you need to embrace your feelings, but manage them at the same time. This can seem very unnatural to learn as an adult, especially if you've spent a lifetime trying to ignore your feelings, stuff them down, or snuff them out.

Your feelings are a healthy part of you, and how you address them and express them can either be a benefit or a detriment to yourself and those around you. All feelings contain important signals and information. The most empowered choice you can make is to use your feelings as a guide toward healing and *not let your feelings use you* to the point that you hurt yourself or others. As you read on, think of your feelings as your gateway to healing and know that how you express those feelings can become the loving evidence of your healing.

Yes, it's hard to face things that happened in your past, take an honest look at what might have been missing in your family of origin, or give up a rosy illusion of a perfect family. But again, this isn't about blame; it's about facing the truth in order to reach a clear understanding, so you can sort out the reasons your invisible hole was formed. Armed with the facts, you don't have to blame yourself or anyone else; you simply put the pieces together to create a better understanding of how the addiction took root in the first place. With that knowledge comes the power to break the emotional patterns that precipitated your addiction.

Here is a three-step process out of fear and toward love. Before you begin, I want to caution you. The process is so simple, you might be inclined to ignore it. Many people get this far, and they think they don't actually need to follow the steps because they're so obvious, so easy. Don't be like I was at first and think you already know how to practice. You can read a book on how to fly a plane, but good luck with actual takeoff and landing. Equally important, these are lifetime exercises— that means you will need to practice them forever. The more you practice, the more skilled you become. Yes, the work is hard, but it's worth it. Stay with it; don't stop.

Step One Toward Love: Face the Pain

Underneath every addiction is old, unaddressed pain. As we discussed earlier, you weren't born addicted. Something happened that created that feeling of an invisible hole, a persistent void. If you find yourself addicted, know that despite your efforts to avoid discomfort and find pleasure, you have sought pleasure and found pain. You might think this sounds crazy, but I assure you it's true. Let's take alcohol as an example. Imagine you had a bad day at work and came home feeling stressed, so you pour yourself a glass of wine, kick off your shoes, sit in your favorite chair, and think with great satisfaction, "Ah! After such a terrible day, I deserve this!"

Fast-forward to when you wake up the next morning still in your favorite chair but with a raging headache, two empty bottles and cocaine wrappers on the floor beside you. Now you are experiencing pain and have set yourself up for another bad day at work—if you can make it there at all. This example illustrates the illusion that perpetuates the addiction loop, but I could have used any addiction pattern to make this point. No matter what substance or activity you choose, the pattern is the same. You turn to the addictive behavior to deal with pain or the void in your life, and as a result, you succeed only in creating more pain and more emptiness, and you don't even realize why. I believe that every addiction reaction is a call for an equal and opposite healing action. If you're addicted, this signifies that you've gone to great lengths to avoid your emotions, and you probably never realized the extent to which you've been rejecting your own feelings until now.

The big problem here is twofold: People are being raised with the messages that emotional pain or discomfort is unacceptable and must be expelled immediately by any means. This belief is what leads to the second piece—choosing self-medicating strategies to try to escape the pain as quickly as possible rather than face it and deal with it.

I've lost several close friends to suicide who would not face their wounds. One was a dear friend who had lived thirty years sober before he ended his life. I'd always worried about him. He attended spirituality seminars and churches with famous upbeat pastors and listened to meditation tapes, but I knew these were only strategies to mask his pain, and he was troubled inside. He could not show his anger or sorrow. I pleaded with him to get help. Sober a long time, he thought he knew what he was doing. He could not see he had transferred his addiction from alcohol and drugs to extreme exercise and spirituality. When his age no longer allowed him to participate in Ironman competitions, and the quotes and affirmations of his spiritual guru no longer generated the endorphins that covered up his wound, he crashed.

The last year of his life, he reenacted the role he'd been put in as a child, an unloved victim. He quit his well-paying job and desperately ran from person to person looking for a place to stay and asking for financial assistance. Many people loved him, but when they offered him real solutions rather than temporary funds or shelter, he refused the help. He kept saying he knew he needed to address his childhood trauma, but when I found him a place to go for help, he told me it just wasn't quite the "right vibe." Several weeks later, consumed by his wound, he hung himself, leaving all of us who cared about him reeling in sorrow. His unwillingness to face his pain cost him his life.

This didn't have to be his end.

Anyone can find a way out. Once you are able to give yourself permission to feel and heal your reactions, you won't need to escape your feelings anymore. You can learn to embrace your emotions, so you won't need to self-medicate. Once you perceive your emotions as a valued aid rather than your enemy, you can give yourself the power to heal.

This self-evaluation questionnaire can assist you in locating the cause of your pain so you can face it.

Self-Evaluation Questionnaire

1. I invite you to think about what you've read thus far. Are you ready to make the commitment to face your pain?

2. What scares you about facing your pain?

3. What are some of the things that cause you to react?

4. If you felt peaceful, without the invisible hole, would you still want to be addicted?

5. Have you ever felt loved, even if briefly? If so, describe that/those experience(s).

6. Have you ever felt love for someone? If so, describe that/those experience(s).

7. Describe how your current relationships resemble your childhood experiences.

Step Two Toward Love: Feel the Pain and Release It

Khalil Gibran wrote that "Your pain is the breaking of the shell that encloses your understanding." I believe this is true, and I've seen it when the addiction can no longer obscure the pain, and it comes spilling out. This outpouring is the beginning of your healing.

When you were young and suffered, you might have learned to close your heart. This action served as a temporary protection against the onslaught of traumatic and painful events. Many of my patients have been able to recall the exact moment they made the decision to emotionally check out. I zoned out at age five when, after an extremely painful moment, I consciously thought, *I don't like it here. I'm never going to feel again.* Throughout my childhood, to protect myself from the cruelty I witnessed and endured, I shut down my heart. It was the only way I knew to temper my suffering.

Shutting down emotionally serves a purpose. It helps a child make it through early life without going insane. Some people disassociate, and when trauma hits, they feel themselves leave their bodies and go through life being observers rather than participants. Regardless of how it happens, once the heart closes, it often stays shut even when it would be safer for it to remain wide open.

Keeping pain out also blocks joy. When my heart was closed, I saw the world in black and white. Even though I lived in one of the most beautiful places, I could not see the living color all around. I went through the motions of life without the emotions. Those who loved me did not get to experience the intimacy they naturally wanted to share with me.

As long as your heart remains closed, you cannot heal. You can go through the motions, but you will not get the results. If you want to heal, the wall must come down. Pain is unavoidable, but when you allow it to wash right through you, love will follow.

There is no safety in a closed heart. You cannot shut out the pain without keeping out the joy. You can't have it both ways. You either go through life like a robot, or you embrace all the sorrow, grief, and broken dreams along with the joy, victories, and fulfilled dreams. With love as your guide, the disappointments will be short-lived and the happiness long.

I like to think of the heart as the emotional recycling center. If your heart is open, you can release your pain, and by the time you're finished crying, your emotions can shift from feelings of heavy gloom to uplifting hope.

Many people have sought spirituality without an open heart, and they accomplish nothing more than a flight of temporary hope that can lead to a crash. Spirituality is found in an open heart, one that feels, one that forgives, one that can love. There is no such thing as a spiritual bypass to love. If you cannot open your heart to loving yourself and others, you cannot expect a magical god or goddess to descend upon you. Remember, you already have all the love you ever need right inside you, and when you share and receive that love with others, you will have found spirituality.

If you're addicted and you're fortunate, at some point your pain will become so great, it will crack open the shell that has kept you separated from the love inside you. In this case pain is a lifesaver. Just as pain in the body tells you something is wrong and needs to be addressed, emotional pain can motivate you to do what you need to do to heal, even if it means getting help. Addressing old pain and trauma alone can be incredibly difficult. If at any point you feel that you need support to help you through the process, or if you are starting to think maybe it's not worth it to continue, make sure you contact a therapist. Getting help is a sign of courage, not weakness. Make sure you see someone trained in mental health and addictions who takes into account the important spiritual component of healing.

When something traumatic happens, feeling pain and loss is natural. However, it doesn't have to lead to or feed addiction. When you allow yourself to feel the pain and grieve, you will naturally heal. But if you refuse to accept a loss that is final by deluding yourself the loss is only temporary, or by suppressing the pain of the loss, you will prolong your suffering, guaranteed.

Elisabeth Kübler-Ross, famous for naming the five stages of a grieving process (denial, anger, bargaining, acceptance, and forgiveness), has helped us better understand how we heal from loss. These stages are normal and natural, and if we move through them all, we can recover from even the most painful losses, at least to the point that we become free of the need to go nuclear. The problem occurs when we resist feeling the grief, and we get stuck in it. Before you can fully recover from addiction, you will need to grieve your unhealed pain.

At first, to deny a traumatic event is normal, as it provides a buffer from shock. Once denial wears off, it's only normal to try to bargain with a higher power or person: "I'll do anything if you'll stop this from happening." It's only natural to feel angry and depressed, because the traumatic event represents a loss of something valued. But when you allow yourself to feel these painful emotions, so you can release them, a new door opens to what the future holds. When you feel your emotions and let them go, it's amazing how fast you can heal the pain of the loss. If you have been unable to grieve because you've never learned how, now is the time.

This step of feeling the pain is the most important part of your healing process, and the most uncomfortable part as well. Many of us have been conditioned by our caretakers to suppress feelings, and we've mastered the ability to shove them down deep. You might dislike feeling vulnerable. You might believe that crying is shameful. You might fear that allowing your emotions to surface and be visible puts an unnecessary burden on others. Many people have told me they are afraid to cry, because once they start, they might never stop. Some have told me they don't allow themselves to get angry anymore, because they have always regretted doing so.

Like any wound, if left unattended, it will only get worse. You can ignore it or numb it, but it won't go away. For example, if you had an addicted parent and you felt abandoned, because it seemed the person was always absent (literally or emotionally), you most likely have attracted people who also leave you with feelings of abandonment. Whenever you feel abandoned by someone now, you might feel powerless to do anything but react. What you do with your reactions can be empowering or debilitating; it's your choice. You can learn to tend to (love) a reactivated wound, so you can stop living with the effects of childhood pain and suffering (fear) and regain emotional stability.

One of my patients attracted men who came on strong, but as soon as the chase was over, they would abruptly back off, leaving her sad and bewildered. When a guy would withdraw, she would try harder to get him back by calling him and catering to his needs, but her neediness would push him even further away. Through therapy, she realized that her reactions were a reenactment of her relationship with an alcoholic father, who was loving and attentive when he was drunk, but solemn and cold when he was not. She was replaying her wound in an unconscious and misguided attempt to reach back in time and receive consistent love from her father. Even though not all of these men were alcoholics like her father, they were all unstable and emotionally inconsistent, stimulating the same feelings of abandonment her father had.

Once she started sitting with her feelings and using the exercises described below to heal her pain, her internal combustion no longer controlled her, no matter how the other person behaved. She was able to recognize her reactions were about her father, not the person in front of her. From a place of neutrality, she was able to do whatever was necessary to take care of herself rather than being at the mercy of her unhealed past, which dictated the same childhood reactions toward the people who reminded her of her alcoholic father.

Another patient, who described his mother as irresponsible (always running late, no organization in the home, no structure), found himself reacting to people who showed similar traits. In a fear-based attempt to keep his wound at bay, he micromanaged his employees. Then, whenever an employee's behavior triggered his unconscious memory of his scatterbrained mother (arriving late, having messy offices, being disorganized), he would blow up and yell at them, which caused further disruption and chaos when the flustered employee would quit. Once he allowed himself to feel the pain and learned how to use his reactions as cues that he needed to engage in self-reflection, he regained his self-control. Rather than suffering the effect of his impulsive reactions, he was able to delegate someone else to address the employee imperfections, and his employees were better able to coalesce as a team rather than be squelched by a frustrated authority figure.

Whatever your reasons for holding in your emotions are, it's time to give them up. All of these reasons only feed the vortex. When you choose love over fear, you are making the decision to purge the pain and replace it with acceptance and peace. Every time you release another part of the pain, you have taken another step out of the maze.

Release the Pain Exercise

Most people who are addicted don't even realize that every time they experience an intense negative emotional reaction, they have reopened an old wound. And every time a new wound occurs, it's like adding a little more TNT to a glass beaker, brewing up the next explosion or "going nuclear." When the compounded emotions from the old wounds surface, feelings of anger, fear, and sorrow arise and create a need to calm those emotions. When the feelings come up then get shoved back down, the inner battle fuels the vortex of pain and expands the invisible hole. Rather than dealing with painful emotions, the addict reenacts the same childhood message that it is not OK to feel. This is the true cause of relapse—the unhealed pain that fuels intense emotional reactions in people who have not been taught how to utilize their emotions in a healthy way.

Here's where you get the opportunity to choose love over fear. It might feel easier to ignore the reaction to try to get rid of your feelings as quickly as possible, or be self-righteous by telling yourself your avoidance is "taking the high road"— these are all examples of choosing fear. You will never get well by ignoring the pain in the vortex or the hollowness of the invisible hole. The decision to face the pain is the choice for love, and when you choose to go about that in a loving way, healing happens.

Remember you are choosing love over fear, so tell yourself you can do this. Every time you do it, you are lifting yourself out of the maze a little further. Instead of ignoring the vortex of pain spinning just beneath the surface of your existence, you can claim these feelings and love yourself through them. Be sure that you do this exercise before you do anything else to relieve the internal tension. As long as you feed the wound with an addiction, you keep the addiction alive. You might not have had a loving person to help you when you were young, but you can be there for yourself now. In fact, if you want to get better, you must be the one that is there for you now.

The technique I am going to describe was taught to me by Michael Singer, when I regularly attended his lectures in Alachua, Florida. For those of you who are interested and would like to know more, Singer wrote *The Untethered Soul.*

The most vital time to use this exercise is when you're aware you're having one of the "nuclear" emotional reactions we spoke of earlier, but you can use this anytime you sense agitation or internal discomfort. No matter what, do this exercise *before* you turn to drink, drugs, food, sex, smoking, or anything else to get rid of the discomfort.

This is not a one-time action. Some of you might have learned this type of technique in therapy or on your own, and as a result, you might believe that you've finished the process. The key to a cure is doing the exercise each and every time you feel a reaction, and you do this for the rest of your life. When I first started doing this process, I felt waves of rage and cried buckets of tears, but now my reactions are only a flicker of emotion. There's no right number of times to do this exercise, only each time another part of your wound surfaces to heal. Depending on the amount of trauma, this might require you to do the exercise ten or a hundred or a thousand times. The point is, you do it as a practice, not as a one-shot "set it and forget it" solution.

First, whenever you notice you are having a *strong emotional reaction that lingers,* no matter what you are doing, go someplace where you can be alone and close your eyes. As soon as possible, remove yourself (even if you have to go into a public bathroom) and do the exercise. (If you are at home, you can download and use the guided meditation on my website, *www.drdonnamarks.com.*)

Once seated, get still, close your eyes, and place your attention on the area of your body where you feel the disturbance. Focus on the internal reaction you are experiencing.

Breathe. Imagine you are watching yourself doing the release exercise and you are safe. Allow all of your feelings to surface. Some people rush through the exercise while having a reaction; they close their eyes for a brief time then nothing happens. The key is to stay in the process until the reaction arises and completely dissipates. You can feel the toxic energy moving and dissipating. Make sure you keep a steady flow of breathing. Holding your breath will block emotions, and prevent your feelings from self-expression.

If you stay committed to this process, you may begin to notice that current events trigger memories of abuse or trauma you've kept buried. These represent the pain that has been bottled up inside most of your life, and they are the roots of your reactions. Allow yourself to feel everything: anger, sadness, fear, or anything else that's going on. While you are feeling these emotions, give yourself a comforting hug, either in your imagination or actually hug yourself. Both are a form of support you may have never received before. Do them and just feel.

With your eyes closed, keep breathing and stay with your feelings until there is nothing left to feel. When the emotional charge has neutralized and a sense of calm comes over you, open your eyes. Singer claims that when the negative feelings are discharged, you will feel the natural joy that has been underneath the pain. Let yourself be quiet for a while, so you can regain your emotional balance.

That's all there is to it, a few simple steps that can provide enormous healing. Just be careful that you don't tell yourself this is so easy that you don't need to go through the simple steps every time your reactions warrant. As long as you continue to do this exercise before you engage in any of your old addictive behaviors, you will remain abstinent, and you can consider yourself cured.

More Ways to Cathect

In addition to the Release the Pain exercise, you can employ other ways to purge toxic feelings. One effective technique is to write out the thoughts and feelings that are disturbing you. This is a healthy way to vent toxic energy without lashing out at someone and harming a relationship. Once you diffuse the negative energy, you can be more open to having a rational conversation. I don't recommend typing your feelings out on your computer. Once someone accidentally copied me on a letter they sent to someone that was full of unpleasantries about me. I didn't mind so much. I feel there are no mistakes in the universe, but it was terribly embarrassing for the other person.

Another technique that I learned and highly recommend to help you release feelings is to write a goodbye letter to someone with whom you have unfinished business. Again, this is not for the purpose of sending it to anyone as it is to benefit your having closure by releasing the pain of unresolved grief. Also, this exercise is equally effective whether the person is alive or not. In the letter, you can recall the good and the bad, how you felt about that person, and the effect they had on you. This is the opportunity to let it all hang out, so don't hold back. Take your time and make a point of getting into as many memories as possible. Make sure you allow all anger, sorrow, remorse, and any other pain to come out. When all of your memories have been purged, end your letter by saying goodbye. Let them know you needed to do this, so you could have closure. When you have nothing else to say, you can tuck the letter away someplace safe, shred it, or find a safe way to burn it as a ceremonial goodbye.

You can continue writing to each and every person with whom you are holding onto unresolved grief. By letting go, you can unlock yourself from old pain and set yourself free to enjoy a new future. Once you have purged the pain associated with your memories of that person, you can encounter this person in a new light, with an unclouded lens from the past.

Choosing love over fear does not mean you need to be perfect. The most important thing is that you keep embracing your emotions and doing the exercise. The cure is a process. You might find yourself engaging in old self-defeating behaviors or even relapsing; this does not mean you are failing. It only means there is more work to do—never give up.

Self-Evaluation Questionnaire

1. If you had been your parent, what would you have done differently?

2. Are you willing to follow those self-designed guidelines now?

3. Do you remember a time that you closed your heart? If so, why?

4. Remember a time that your heart was open. What did that feel like?

5. If your heart is closed, how does that block you from healing your pain?

6. Are you willing to go through a short-term process of letting your heart open, so it can cleanse your pain? Describe what that would look like.

7. Write down any concerns you have about feeling your pain and how you can comfort yourself.

Step Three Toward Love: Forgive the Pain

A Course in Miracles tells us, "Forgiveness is the key to happiness." Let that sink in.

Without forgiveness, your healing cannot be complete. The ego tells us we are foolish to forgive, but when you've chosen love, holding onto resentments is perceived as boring and unproductive. You learn there is no value in keeping a wound alive, and you are much better off feeling the pain, releasing it, and letting go of the anger and resentment. Whatever the cause of your pain—loss of a loved one, loss of pride, financial loss—it doesn't matter; it's all the same. To heal, we must forgive.

Remember, *A Course in Miracles* defines a miracle as "a change in perception." Many people change their perception of childhood abuse from anger and hurt to compassion and forgiveness. They begin to see that the person who hurt them was sick. One patient who had been physically and sexually abused told me, "I actually felt sorry for my dad. He had to live with what he did to me. I think it ate him alive, and that's why he drank all the time."

Forgiveness allows us to stop dragging around the heavy load of long-ago events. Hanging onto old baggage would be like writing a giant book about every bad memory of your life then lugging it around wherever you went. It would always be there, slowing you down, tiring you out. You'd drag it out of bed with you in the morning and into bed with you at night. You'd work, dance, and make love with a 100-pound book strapped to you at all times. Not much fun. Now that your wound is healing, you can finish each chapter and put it on a shelf called "My Life." You no longer carry the heavy load around, yet the stories will remain an important part of who you are, not what you are.

When new reactions emerge, your practice is to continue to purge your charged emotions. You feel your pain and release it and let go of those bad stories one at a time. Every time a part of the wound heals, the load is a little lighter, and life gets easier. One morning you wake up without any baggage at all, able to feel lighthearted and look forward to the day—full of happiness.

Let Go of Resentment

It's not always easy to forgive someone who caused you great harm, but it's in your best interests to do so. When your invisible hole is carrying residuals of resentment, your healing is not complete. When you make the choice to love yourself, there's no place for resentments; love cannot live where resentments reside.

Part of loving yourself is remaining free of toxic thoughts and feelings. Some people think that keeping up a wall offers protection from further hurt or betrayal, but this is not true. Resentments only maintain barriers that keep you in the maze, just as the unhealthy ego wants.

I'm not suggesting that we excuse unacceptable behavior, but rather (as *A Course in Miracles* suggests) to look at it differently. There's no freedom in blaming people who were not well enough to provide a healthy template. Most abusers were abused as children and are too sick or ashamed to learn a better way. Maybe someday more parents will take classes that teach good parenting skills. Meanwhile, for those of us who were abused or became perpetrators ourselves, our greatest hope of change is through healing our painful past and through forgiveness. When we forgive, we lift the veil of shame and allow ourselves to open up to permanent healing.

One of the most important concepts *A Course in Miracles* offers is that underneath every unforgiven thought toward someone else is self-condemnation. When I first read this, I could not wrap my mind around it. It seemed so ridiculous. I wondered how a little child could feel responsible for being abused. But then I thought back to my own childhood, and I remembered thinking, what did I do to cause him to hurt me? Only five years old and emotionally crushed by a stepfather I loved, it had to be my fault that such raging hatred was cast upon me. Later, when healing my emotional wounds, I better understood *A Course in Miracles*. I blamed myself, and I had taken over the role of beating myself up when no one else was.

As adults, we can notice how beneath our grievances, there are always feelings of inadequacy. "I should have been smarter," "I shouldn't have trusted him or her," and "I should have listened to my gut" are typical comments that accompany resentment. We cannot expect ourselves to be perfect, it's easy to trust the wrong people, and everyone makes mistakes.

One patient, Herman, was a recovering alcoholic and addict, who, while in a workshop I was teaching, uncovered the root of his addiction. Herman had never shared his secret with anyone, and when he calmly unveiled the trauma that led to his addiction, it shocked all of us. When he was about six years old, Herman's parents had left him with his two-year-old brother at a fountain while his parents went to the restroom. When they returned, Herman was sitting on the side of the fountain daydreaming. When his parents asked him where his little brother was, he realized he'd forgotten all about him. Tragically, his little brother had fallen in the fountain and drowned.

Herman's parents blamed him for his brother's death, causing him to feel ashamed. Herman also blamed himself for his brother's drowning, and he used alcohol and drugs to escape the pain he felt. His life had become a long ordeal of silent suffering, and now in the group, he courageously shared his secret for the first time. The compassion of the other members helped him release years of pent-up pain through gut-wrenching sobs and wails. But the real miracle occurred when, for the first time, Herman was able to see that it was not he who was at fault, but his parents who'd made the mistake of leaving an infant in the care of another child. At that point, Herman was able to free himself from blame then understand that his parents had paid dearly for their own poor judgment, and no one needed to bear the cross of human failure any longer.

A Course in Miracles teaches us that we are not sinners; we are merely human beings, and we all make mistakes. Rather than condemn ourselves, we need to simply acknowledge our "errors" and do what we can to correct them. But the unhealthy ego uses guilt to keep us in a state of feeling unworthy. As we discussed earlier, guilt rarely stops us from doing something we are intent on doing—especially an addictive behavior. Remember, guilt and anger only cover up our fears and lead us to believe we won't be happy without our pseudo comfort. But the addiction provides only short-term relief for long-term misery, and it reinjures us. The invisible hole is never filled, and the suffering continues.

If you want out of the maze, you must find and fill the invisible hole with love and positive esteem for yourself. When you have forgiven yourself and others and let love in, that love will replace your need for the addiction. You will no longer need an external fix for something that is readily available within.

You will no longer need to substitute an addiction for love because your choice for love is the cure.

Visualize Your New Life

Another powerful technique is to visualize yourself as healthy, healed, and out of the maze of addiction. I invite you to take some time to picture your ideal life free from addiction. How do you see yourself living? What experiences will you have? Will you wake up feeling excited about the day? Will your life have added meaning and a sense of purpose? Would you be engaged in helping others? Would you enjoy time alone, more time with friends, a mixture of both? What hobbies would you be loving? Would you have a romantic relationship that felt safe and enriching to both people? What would your home look like decorated in your own personal taste? Would you have any new pets? A garden? What would you be doing for fun? What lifelong dreams would you be fulfilling? How will you handle disappointment, setbacks, and loss? I think this is one of the most important questions, as the way you learn to handle life's bumps can say more about your healing than how you handle the times when things are going great.

One patient who'd gone through this three-step process and had suffered a great deal of pain after a divorce, described his exit from the maze:

A few weeks ago, I was stuck in my apartment alone during a storm. I could have called someone. I didn't; instead I decided to do what I've learned—face the pain and feel it. The pain crept over me, like a dark ghost, telling me all kinds of things: you're a loser; what the hell is the matter with you? I remembered hearing that same question throughout my childhood. Back then, it drove me to success; now, when all my efforts would not produce marital success, it crushed me. I sat with the feelings of failure as each day drew darker. I was alone, so alone. I felt like I was falling in a hole, and I let it consume me. I wasn't sure if I would live or die. Then one morning I awoke, I looked out of the window and saw the sky. I heard the waves, the sounds of seagulls, and the smell of coffee brewing. I wasn't alone anymore. I was here, with myself, and beauty was all around me. Family photos, a nice home, my favorite books, a file on the desk full of lifetime awards, art, *A Course in Miracles* book beside me. I now have the peace I've never felt before. I love my life. I'm glad I didn't give up; it's been a difficult process, and there was so much to release, to heal. Now when I watch other couples fighting and they're not able to connect, for the first time in my life, I'm glad to be alone. I've found peace. I'm grateful for the marriage and the divorce; they brought up the deeper wounds I never had the courage to face. Had I not been addicted to her, I would have kept old trauma safely at bay, along with all the love I feel, including the compassion I feel for her, that has replaced the anger and resentment. Someday, I will meet someone. Right now, I'm on a different journey of loving myself and the world around me.

You, too, can find the peace you were intended to have. You can save yourself years of "searching but never finding." A child in pain has few choices. It's not possible for children to leave an abusive or neglectful home without risking death in the outside world, though in some cases they might be safer out there than at home. But now that you are no longer a child, you can choose to make your own rules—you get to choose love over fear. Answering the following questions can help you identify areas of your life where you have not forgiven so you can begin to forgive the people and events that precipitated your original pain. Once you forgive, you are out of the maze. To stay out, you will have to keep letting go and choosing love.

Self-Evaluation Questionnaire

1. Do you hold resentments toward someone else that you haven't been able to shake off?

2. How have those resentments benefited you?

3. Make a list of everyone you haven't forgiven and why.

4. Looking at each situation, write down how you might have blamed yourself.

5. Write a letter to each person, including yourself. Expel all of your pain and anger, then either shred the letter or burn it, letting it all go.

6. Write a letter to yourself as though you were a loving parent, forgiving yourself for being less than perfect.

Remind yourself you are human, and humans make mistakes. Tell yourself that you are loved, and that the more you learn to love yourself, the more loved you will feel.

CHAPTER TWELVE

EXIT THE MAZE FOR GOOD

Freedom is not worth having if it does not include the
freedom to make mistakes.
—Mahatma Gandhi

You've exited the maze; now here are some strategies for continuing your self-care so you remain cured. Life is not perfect, it has its ups and downs, and if you stay addiction-free, you can learn how to grow with the imperfections in yourself and others. If you remember to choose to love rather than harm, you will be able to sustain the happiness that replaces any need for self-destructive addiction, even when you screw up.

One of my favorite teachings in *A Course in Miracles* is: "There are no sins, only mistakes." Mistakes are part of being human, and "All things are lessons God would have you learn." Now that you've come this far, remember that it's only natural you will make mistakes along the way. Give yourself permission to be human. When you make mistakes, use them to learn, so you can grow from them rather than staying stuck in guilt and shame.

When patients relapse, they tell me how awful they feel. My intent is that they not waste precious time and energy beating themselves up, so I encourage them to explore what happened prior to the relapse. Most of the time they were triggered by an emotional reaction. I remind them that this is an opportunity to locate the unresolved pain that caused the reaction and release it, so they aren't triggered again.

When you give yourself permission to make mistakes, and you make the effort to understand why, you pave the way to make a more loving choice next time. Generally, any mistake you make will do far less damage than the reaction to the mistake if you beat yourself up. Don't let mistakes get you down; hold your head up high and choose love rather than relapse when you're tempted to castigate yourself or numb out.

When you stumble, get support from people who can help you, especially someone who's been where you are and knows what you're going through. Another way to love yourself through your mistakes is to talk to yourself as if you were a young person who just screwed up. Rather than shaming that little person, you could say something like, "It's OK to make mistakes. I am not mad at you. I don't expect you to be perfect, and I love you no matter what. We can talk about what happened, then you can do better next time."

Ways to Love Yourself

You are the most important person you will ever love. If you've been addicted, we can safely assume that you either received too little or too much of the loving ingredients that would make you feel whole and self-sufficient.

Giving up something, even if it's not good for you, must be replaced with something that is good for you. Remember, that hole formed long ago; now that you're in healing mode, you will need to replace that void with love. Think of filling the invisible hole as a daily practice of self-love and self-care, not too much or too little. Love is all around you. Love will not intrude upon you or force its way through your walls. If you want the cure, you have to let it in.

Remember that the cure is an ongoing process, and you always have the freedom to choose love over addiction. You are retraining your brain to replace self-destructive acts with acts of love. Every time you choose to treat yourself with love, you are rebuilding self-trust. It feels awful to be told that you're loved then get treated like crap, so be sure that as you pledge your love to yourself, you treat yourself well.

I'm going to make some suggestions on how to love yourself. You can also create your own strategies and safeguards to help you continue to choose love. I've placed some questions at the end of the chapter you can use as a guide to get started.

Care for Your Time

Every moment of every day is a gift. Joy and happiness are natural and not things to waste time pursuing. You are here for a reason; give your life the chance it deserves; it awaits you. There are two doors: One says LOVE, one says FEAR, one leads to heaven, the other to hell. It's up to you. I suspect if you've read this far, whether you realize it or not, you've made the decision for love. *A Course in Miracles* states: "Love waits on welcome, not on time." This moment is as important as any other; your dreams await you. I suspect, deep down you have a lifelong vision for your life; you know what it is, so let it unfold. It's very easy—one addiction, one cure, and one path to freedom. The sooner you open your heart, the sooner your life will bloom.

Care for Your Body

Care for your body as if you were caring for a young child. In addition to the things we outlined under the section on healthy parenting, you can do more. This means that you eat to live, not live to eat. Instead of going for fast food, go for good food. Avoid putting toxins in your body and toxic people in your brain.

Give your body the exercise it needs to stay fit, but without fixating on having a perfect body—another invisible hole that has no end. You can give your body the sleep it needs to stay rested, listening to what it tells you. Take the time for pampering, but for the purpose of feeling good on the inside, not just to look good on the outside. During times of stress, you can double-down on all of these strategies.

Enjoy hobbies and interests that balance with your work and free time. Make friends with people who have your back, not a knife in your back. Prepare for success, lay out a plan, then wait for its arrival. Many plans derail when they are forced to happen too soon.

Care for Your Spirit

Listen to yourself and trust your spirit—your internal navigation system. Take time to commune with beauty—sunsets, the sounds of nature, walks in the fresh air, beautiful music—and ground yourself in your responsibilities. Deeply inhale the scent of roses and all the perfume of nature. Spend time in solitude to listen to your higher consciousness while you keep both feet firmly planted on the ground.

Allow yourself to be fascinated with everything around you. Life keeps regenerating itself, and every single thing that you see—your clothes, computers, dishes, furniture, jewelry, windows—they all came out of the ground; imagine that. All creation has made our lives easier. We don't know what it would be like to live in caves and fend against wild animals for food; we take so much for granted. Gratitude is the circuitry to keep you plugged into this creative life force.

All the love you want and need is right inside of you, and your commitment to that inward journey is what will keep you out of the maze forever.

Care for Your Relationships

Allowing people to love you is an important part of self-love. We are not supposed to be isolated unto ourselves; we are designed to share and receive love with others. *A Course in Miracles* teaches, "Sharing and receiving are the same." The loving relationships you develop offer opportunities to share and receive love and add fulfillment and satisfaction to life. Many people have been so hurt that they are afraid to trust anyone. If that's how you feel, you can start to realize that you are the most important person you will ever trust. As long as you forgive and keep an open heart, you can overcome any amount of pain. Going forward, if you will listen to your Holy Spirit and trust it, you won't have to be hurt as much because you will receive the protective suggestions offered to you. If bad things do happen, you can use the tools you now have to work through the pain without self-destructing. When you nurture yourself through the grief, you will learn to trust that you can heal no matter what.

When you come from love, you can practice balancing your wants and needs with those of others, and by negotiating those mutual needs, you can build sustainable relationships. This is what I call the "We Program," as opposed to the "Me Program." You aren't afraid of losing someone if you express your own desires, and you make yourself more authentic to the other person. At the same time, you put your loving actions to your words by caring about the other's wants and needs as much as your own.

Care for Your Mind

Pause when agitated and act when you are calm. There's no shame in getting help if you need it, but you don't have to entrust your mind to just anyone or any facility. Make sure the people who help you are compassionate and competent. Like any relationship, be choosy and make sure it's a good fit.

Listen to your intuitive mind and allow yourself to develop trust with that part of you. Treasure your memories and, like a garden, allow the good memories to represent the flora and the weeds of sorrow to wilt and die.

Allow your mind to be open but wise. If something sounds good, but doesn't feel right, make sure the two are aligned before you go forward. Be aware of the ego, the part of the mind that is always waiting to steer you off course. If this happens, you will feel uneasy, and at any time, you can reconnect to the voice of the Holy Spirit.

When Fear Arises

It's only natural that fear will creep into your mind. When you feel empty, lonely, or restless, remember that loving yourself allows you to recognize any discomfort as an indication you need to give yourself love—the healthy nurturing and attention you need. Whether you cuddle with a blanket and pillow, fix yourself a cup of hot tea or your favorite (healthy) meal, talk to a loved one, engage in your favorite hobby, listen to music, meditate or commune with your Holy Spirit, or just sit and be, you can do these things to recharge your tank with love.

You also can use affirmations. One of my favorites is: "I have all the love I need, I am healing, I am not alone, and I have many good things in my life now." Another favorite: "I'm uncomfortable, but I'm growing fast. It's all good, even if I don't like it." The key to using affirmations effectively is to try to feel them deep in your heart and not just say the words. Love is always there for you to call upon. Like anything else, the more you practice choosing love over fear, the better off you are. Whenever you are not at peace, embrace the discomfort and call on love to help you. The answers will come, and they will feel right.

The Hearts Exercise

I'm going to share with you an exercise people in my workshops enjoy doing; it can be a metaphor for how to fill the invisible hole. Even middle-aged men in their fifties and older who thought this exercise was silly received great joy when they followed the steps.

Buy yourself a good-size clear glass jar and a pad of red construction paper and a pad of black. Cut the black paper into strips and wad them up. Put all of them in the jar. Cut hearts out of the red construction paper. Every time you do something good for yourself, such as walk away from a temptation, embrace your feelings, help someone, take a hot bath, make a good decision, or any other loving act, take out a black wad and put in a red heart. After a while, you will be amazed how your red hearts have replaced the black strips. This can be an ongoing visual reminder of how much you are changing through learning to love yourself.

Cherish Your Inner Newborn

One last exercise. If you have a picture of when you were a baby, pull it out; if not, you can go ahead without one. I invite you to go back to your birth and have an imaginary conversation with that newborn baby, you, who came into the world on the day of your birth. You just left a warm, safe place to come somewhere totally strange and foreign. Look at how precious you are, how innocent, vulnerable, and dependent on the world around you. You know nothing about rules and regulations; the only need you have right now is to be cared for and loved.

Look deeply into that baby's eyes and show the love that you have. Tell that baby how happy you are with their arrival and how you will take good care of that baby now. Hold the baby warmly in your arms, safe and secure. Kiss the soft downy head and send it all the love you've ever felt. Let the baby know you are always here. You are in charge now and can be trusted. You are listening, you care, you will do your best, and when you fall short, you will do better next time. Tell the baby how much you love him or her and feel the joy of new life, feel the connection to that newborn, you. Never let go. Carry that little one in your heart forever.

Every time you choose love, you are choosing the gift of life now, and in that choice, love will continue to bloom. Love is in you and all around you. Love is the only answer; love is the only cure.

Self-Evaluation Questionnaire

The following questions are designed to help you come up with your own ideas for ways to love yourself.

1. When you were little, what made you feel loved?

2. Which of those ways do you still do?

3. List some new ways you can show love to yourself.

4. Is there anything that would stop you from creating a new healthy template?

5. If you had a healthy template now, what would that look like?

6. How would you compare love with spirituality?

7. Create some strategies and safeguards to prevent relapse.

    A. Write down three affirmations to use when you're tempted to do the unloving things.

    B. Write down a gratitude list you can read when you feel a sense of lack.

    C. Make a list of people who are safe support for you.

    D. Review the exercise on feeling and releasing pain. Write down the steps.

    E. Write down three positive things you will do when you make a mistake.

8. Describe your future self (or present self) who is happy and fulfilled. Where do you live? Who are you with? What does your day look like? Describe your home, your friends, your career (if any), your favorite pastimes. What is bringing you the most joy? Describe how you keep yourself free from pain and in the place of love.

LOVE AWAITS

So many of us get bogged down in the mirages of life, and we miss the reasons we are here—to share and receive love. As you go forward, my wish is that you experience the miraculous change in perception that there is little to fear and much to love. When you look at life through the eyes of love, love will shine back at you. When you are choosing love, it is impossible to treat yourself in a way that is harmful. When you choose love, you forgive your mistakes and lovingly correct them.

I would like to offer you one final challenge. For one month, follow the steps outlined in this book and see if you improve. You can always go back to the old way, but I suspect, once you get a taste of real love for yourself, the attraction for poor substitutes will lose their appeal to you.

You never have to be imprisoned in the hell maze again. You won't have to worry about trying to control anything, because if you have to control it, it's not good for you, and you won't want it. When you are free, you can be happy no matter what is going on, because you know how to love yourself and others through any conflict or problem. When you have been in the maze of addiction then healed the invisible hole, that black hole will fill with light and guide you to all the love you could ever want. Even in your darkest times, if you go within to find even an inkling of that love, you will have recaptured a spark of your birthright for a happy, joyous life. Once that happens, the thought of putting yourself back in addiction prison will lose all of its appeal, not because you are afraid of addiction, but because it feels so much better to love yourself and enjoy your life than to tolerate harming your body or bogging down your mind with all the yucky feelings that follow relapse.

If you have chosen to exit the maze, you have already chosen the one cure, and you are on the path to freedom. Love is in you. You can enjoy the journey to find it. There is no better destination. All you have ever wanted and needed has been with you your entire life, right inside your very own heart. Go there now. Love awaits.

ABOUT THE AUTHOR

Dr. Donna Marks believes that the current models for diagnosis, treatment, and addiction have failed. Her mission is to help save at least 10 million lives by 2030 through education and prevention. She has been an author, consultant, educator, public speaker, licensed psychotherapist and addiction counselor in private practice in Palm Beach, Florida for more than thirty years.

In addition to seeing patients, she teaches *A Course in Miracles*, facilitates workshops, and has a strong media presence. Using both her professional expertise and her life-long experience with her personal recovery and healing, Dr. Marks is best known for her work in preventing and treating addictions. She combines psychoanalytic methodologies and spiritual concepts to help people get at the real cause and cure for addiction.

Dr. Mark's clientele has ranged from the homeless to the wealthy and famous. In 1986, she co-owned an out-patient treatment program that was one of the first to incorporate a patient's entire family (including young children) in the addiction recovery process. She also has served as an advisor to treatment centers and on several mental health and addictions treatment boards.

In 1989, Dr. Marks developed a chemical dependency treatment program at Palm Beach Community College that has since grown into a four-year degree program, for which she was given *An Award of Appreciation* by the College. She has also received the *Peter Fairclough Award for Service in the Field of Recovery,* and a *Mobilization for Action through Planning & Partnerships Community Service Award* by the Governor's Council for Community Health Partnerships.

No stranger to adversity, Dr. Marks was a single mom at the age of eighteen and a high school dropout. She obtained her G.E.D. degree by attending night school, then went on to earn an Associate's Degree, a Bachelor's Degree, and a Master's Degree in Psychology. She became licensed as a Mental Health Counselor in 1987. In 1989, she earned a Doctorate Degree in Adult Education, then became a Certified Addictions Professional, Certified Gestalt Therapist, Certified Psycho-analyst, Hypnotherapist, and Certified Sex Therapist.

A mother of three grown children, she lives with her husband in West Palm Beach, Florida.

Learn more about Dr. Marks, her books and services at www.DrDonnaMarks.com.

Free Bonus

Would you like more information on healing addiction?

Do you have trouble accessing your feelings?

Dr. Marks is offering a free meditation to help with this.

You can also watch her videos on addiction and her *Course in Miracles* classes.

Want more than a book?
You can sign up for an online course,
Exit the Maz: One Addiction, One Cause, One Cure,
to help accelerate your healing process.

For more information
and to access this bonus and videos,
please visit **www.drdonnamarks.com**

Made in United States
North Haven, CT
05 March 2022

16826297R00117